THE FAR HORIZON

Perspectives on Life Beyond Death

MICHAEL PRESCOTT

www.whitecrowbooks.com

The Far Horizon: Perspectives on Life Beyond Death,
by Michael Prescott

Published in the United States of America and the United Kingdom by White Crow Books, an imprint of White Crow Productions Ltd.

A CIP catalogue record for this book is available from the British Library

For information: e-mail info@whitecrowbooks.com.

Cover photo by Marilyn Volan
D 5620978 © Marilyn Volan | Dreamstime.com

Interior design by Velin@Perseus-Design.com

Paperback: ISBN: 978-1-78677-145-2
eBook: ISBN: 978-1-78677-146-9

Non Fiction / Spiritualism / Parapsychology / Death & Dying

"Only he who keeps his eye fixed on the far horizon will find the right road."

—Dag Hammarskjöld

A NOTE ON THE TEXT

IN LIEU OF footnotes, I've briefly incorporated the source of any quotation into the text, either by crediting the author and title before the quote, or by placing the author's last name and an abbreviated title in parentheses after the quote. More complete information is provided in the bibliography.

A few asides that didn't fit neatly into the main body of the book are included in the chapter notes at the end.

M.P.

CONTENTS

INTRODUCTION	p. 9
CHAPTER ONE: THE FIRST MODEL	p. 38
CHAPTER TWO: THE SECOND MODEL	p. 79
CHAPTER THREE: THE THIRD MODEL	p. 120
CHAPTER FOUR: THE FOURTH MODEL	p. 147
EPILOGUE: THE I-THOUGHT	p. 174
CHAPTER NOTES	p. 184
ACKNOWLEDGMENTS	p. 194
BIBLIOGRAPHY	p. 197

INTRODUCTION

ON OCTOBER 5, 1930, at 2:05 in the morning, the 777-foot British dirigible R-101 crashed in flames in the woods near the French town of Beauvais, en route to India. All of the passengers and most of the crew perished, and British airship production suffered a setback from which it never recovered.

Two days later, the London medium Eileen Garrett, while in a trance, began to convey messages purporting to come from Lieutenant H.C. Irwin, who died aboard the R-101. In jerky, staccato utterances typical of his speech pattern in life, "Irwin" said, "The whole bulk of the dirigible was entirely and absolutely too much for her engine capacity. Engines too heavy. It was this that on five occasions made me scuttle back to safety ... Useful lift too small. Gross lift computed badly ... Explosion caused by friction in electric storm. Flying too low altitude and could never rise. Disposable lift could not be utilized ..."

The voice went on, speaking almost faster than the stenographer at the session could take it down.

Over the next few months, Eileen Garrett continued to receive communications from Irwin and other R-101 crew members, as recounted in detail by John G. Fuller in *The Airmen Who Would Not Die*. While the first séance took place in the presence of psychic researcher Harry Price, the remaining ones involved a different sitter, Major Oliver Villiers, himself a friend of Irwin and an expert in aviation (though not in the field of dirigible design). Included in the messages were technical details about the R-101's design and construction, recollections of test flights, discussions of political pressures and unrealistic deadlines that plagued the project, and a description of the crash itself and its causes. The personalities of the dead airmen came through in recognizable detail. In one instance Villiers asked the communicating entity to identify itself, at which point the voice replied, "Use your damned intelligence!"—a catch phrase used by a crewman who died in the crash.

Indeed, the personalities of the men emerged so clearly that Villiers, who had several sessions with Garrett, eventually fell into conversing with his old friends as if they were in the room with him.

Garrett's séances, held in broad daylight in a room designed by Harry Price to be a sealed, deceit-proof environment, yielded so much detailed, factual information that Villiers was moved to present the transcripts to Sir John Simon, in charge of the government's investigation into the crash. This was a bold decision on Villiers' part, one that could have jeopardized his career if Simon had looked unkindly on the idea of combing through the transcripts of séances for clues. Yet Simon handled the material respectfully and followed up on leads suggested by the communications.

Working independently of Villiers, Harry Price had the transcript of his single session with Garrett analyzed by Will Charlton, supply officer at Cardington, where the R-101 was built and tested. Charlton, though not an engineer himself, knew all the engineers who had built and tested the airship. He shared the transcript with them, obtaining their input.

His meticulous analysis revealed that most of the information in the initial session was accurate.

"Irwin" said: "The whole bulk of the dirigible was entirely and absolutely too much for her engine capacity ... Engines too heavy ... Useful lift too small ... Gross lift computed badly." All of these comments were correct.

"Flying too low altitude and could never rise ... Disposable lift could not be utilized ... Load too great for long flight." Many witnesses observed that the R-101 was flying low. The ship dumped half its ballast just to escape from the mooring tower, and heavy rain that night would have added more weight to the vessel.

"Weather bad for long flight ... Fabric all waterlogged and ship's nose is down ... Impossible to rise ... Cannot trim ... Almost scraped the roofs at Achy." The trip took place in a driving rainstorm with high winds. The R-101 was seen flying with its nose angled downward. Charlton noted, "Achy is a small village, 12 ½ miles north of Beauvais, and would be on the R-101's route."

Much of the information was outside the province of any layman.

"Irwin" said: "Starboard strakes started." The word *strakes* is a technical term originally used in shipbuilding. Irwin had a naval background. .

"Airscrews too small." Charlton felt that this was likely to be correct, and noted that the airscrews used on the R-101 were smaller than those originally planned.

"Next time with cylinders but bore of engine 1,100 cc's ..." Charlton noted that this would be correct if the term *cubic inches* was substituted for *cubic centimeters* ("cc's").

"... the bore capacity was entirely inadequate to the volume of structure." Charlton noted: "This language is technically correct and *might* have been Irwin's opinion. It is an opinion that could only be expressed by an expert in the subject."

"... it will be found that the superstructure of the envelope contained no resilience and had far too much weight." Charlton found this accurate, saying, "It was the most rigid airship that had ever been constructed."

"The added middle section was entirely wrong. It made strong, but took resilience away and entirely impossible. Too heavy and too much overweighted for the capacity of the engines." The R-101 had been expanded to 777 feet by the addition of a new "middle section" only a few months before the flight. This addition greatly complicated the craft's handling and may well have contributed to the crash.

In some instances, the information was unknown to anyone who had not been part of the Cardington team.

"Irwin": "This exorbitant scheme of carbon and hydrogen is entirely and absolutely wrong." This appears to be a reference to upcoming experiments involving a mixture of oil fuel ("carbon") and hydrogen. These experiments, in the planning stage at Cardington shortly before the R-101's crash, were not reported in the press; only project team members, like Irwin, knew about them.

"Too short trials ... No one knew the ship properly." The abbreviated test period was a concern of those working at Cardington, but was unknown to the public at the time of the séance.

"It was this that made me on five occasions have to scuttle

back to safety." True—Irwin had cut short several test flights because the ship was too heavy. The press had not been told of these failures.

Villiers' notes, which were not seen by Charlton, offered an equal wealth of technical detail, as well as personal observations. Among these was the claim by a voice representing itself as another crew member, Lieutenant Commander Atherstone, that he had kept a secret diary recording his worries about the R-101 program. When official inquiries were made of his widow regarding this diary, she insisted she had never heard of it. But years later, in 1967, Mrs. Atherstone produced the diary, which was found to contain exactly the kinds of private worries mentioned by the "Atherstone" voice nearly four decades earlier.

Skeptics were unpersuaded. Wing Commander Booth, captain of a similar airship, the R-100, considered the reported conversations to be "completely out of character, the atmosphere at Cardington ... completely wrong ...'" Yet Charlton and Villiers, who worked at Cardington and knew the crew members, assessed the conversations quite differently. And there does not seem to be any doubt that "the atmosphere at Cardington" was one of political infighting, impossible deadlines, and desperate shortcuts, just as the messages suggest.

Booth also claimed that the messages' technical information "could not possibly have come from anyone with airship experience." But equally knowledgeable aviation experts like Lord Dowding, commander-in-chief of the (British) Fighter Command in World War II, and Sir Victor Goddard, former commander of the Royal New Zealand Air Force, were favorably impressed with the technical accuracy of the messages.

Admittedly, some details conveyed in the séances were wrong. Villiers distinctly heard mention of "altimeter springs" on two occasions, but the R-101's altimeters had no springs. "Irwin" mentioned a gas indicator rising and falling throughout the flight, but Booth says that there was no such gauge on board.

Most of the information, however, appears to have been correct. Garrett's statements about the crash were sufficiently accurate to arouse the suspicion of the British government, which sent agents to investigate the medium on the chance that she had been in collusion with someone at Cardington. No link between her and the airship project was uncovered. This is hardly surprising, since Garrett traveled in very different circles from the R-101's crewmen and engineers. As a member of London's literary arts community, she numbered among her friends such luminaries as James Joyce and George Bernard Shaw. There is no evidence of any overlap between the literary and theatrical circle in which she moved and the tight-knit fraternity of engineering experts working on a secret government project.

Nor was she an engineering whiz who could have inferred the technical details from oblique references in the newspapers, as some have rather desperately suggested. Though brilliant in many ways, Garrett had no mechanical abilities and never even learned to drive a car.

Another objection was that, according to the séances, the crew members knew they were setting off on a suicidal mission, when in reality they had no such foreknowledge. But in fact, more than one crew member expressed serious reservations about the test flight. One of them told Villiers at the time, "I have had several talks with [other crewmen]. They've become more and more uneasy at the prospect of this journey to India. In their opinion, the ship is not really airworthy." The Atherstone diary confirms that the R-101 crew were well aware of the risks of the flight.

If they were so concerned, why take the trip at all? This objection was answered in the séances themselves, when it was explained that, for political purposes, it was thought necessary to start the much-ballyhooed trip to India by crossing the English Channel. The airship could then be docked in France, and the cancellation of the rest of the trip could be blamed on bad weather. This compromise was a way of saving face, both for the British government, which had invested two million pounds sterling in the project, and for the R-101 program itself, which was dependent on political goodwill for continued funding.

The scheme, while desperate, was not necessarily "suicidal." In fact, the airship did make its way across the Channel before suffering irreparable damage. Had the forecast of twenty- to thirty-knot winds proved accurate, the R-101 probably would have docked safely in France. Unfortunately, the winds blew at forty to fifty knots, conditions the crew could not have anticipated when starting out.

In February of 1892, George Pellew, his vision clouded by an eye infection, fell through an open grate on a Manhattan street. He died instantly. He was thirty-two years old. A graduate of Harvard Law, he had written several books, including a memoir of his travels in Ireland, an argument for women's suffrage, a study of Jane Austen, and a biography of

John Jay, his great-grandfather.

A little more than four weeks after his death, Pellew apparently made an appearance at a séance with the Boston medium Leonora Piper, who was being closely studied by the Society for Psychical Research. The two sitters, James and Mary Hart, had been acquainted with Pellew. According to the SPR's chief investigator, Richard Hodgson, the couple received "strongly personal specific references." And then

> in connection with Mrs. Howard [a mutual friend] came the name Katharine. "Tell her, she'll know, I will solve the problems, Katharine." Mr. Hart notes: "This had no special significance for me at the time ... On the day following the sitting I gave Mr. Howard a detailed account of the sitting. These words, 'I will solve the problems, Katharine,' impressed him more than anything else, and at the close of my account he related that George, when he had last met with them, had talked frequently with Katharine (a girl of fifteen years of age) upon such subjects as Time, Space, God, and Eternity, and pointed out to her how unsatisfactory the commonly accepted solutions were. He added that some time he would solve the problems, and let her know." (Myers, *Human Personality*)

Hodgson, who had known Pellew fairly well, was encouraged by these early results and intrigued by the prospect of testing a spirit who claimed to be someone familiar to him. To do so, he devised a new experimental strategy. As Pulitzer

Prize-winning science writer Deborah Blum tells us,

> Hodgson began by making a list of old friends and family members of the dead writer. He would invite them, as many as would agree, to come anonymously and check their knowledge against that of the trance personality ...
>
> His investigation of the so-called ghost of George Pellew was based upon a simple idea, with a twist. He would bring more than a hundred visitors, eventually, to sit with Mrs. Piper. Some would be friends of the dead man; some would be strangers to him. But she would be given no relationship clues. No participants would be allowed to tell their names or whether they had any connection to G.P. [as Pellew was typically known in the sittings]. They would be allowed to improvise personal tests, but they would not be allowed to give any explanation for them.
>
> One visitor brought a photograph of a building.
>
> "Do you recognize this?"
>
> "Yes, it is your summer house."
>
> Which it was.
>
> Another woman placed a book on the medium's head.
>
> "Do you recognize this?" she said to G.P.
>
> "My French lyrics," he answered.
>
> That was right too.
>
> Another visitor, a man, simply asked, "Tell me something, in our past, that you and I alone know."
>
> As he spoke, Mrs. Piper sat slumped forward into

a pile of pillows on the table, her left hand dangling limply over the edge, her right hand coiled loosely around the pencil. Next to her right side, a pad of paper sat on the table. Suddenly, her fingers tightened and she began to write, wildly, filling pages, ripping them off, thrusting them away from her.

Hodgson moved to the other side of the room. The man began flipping through the pages. He paled and folded the papers. They were too private to read aloud, he told Hodgson.

But he was "perfectly satisfied, perfectly."...

After sittings with 130 different visitors, [Hodgson had] been persuaded of the impossible—that the personality in the room was indeed a spirit, proof that his friend lived on.

Out of that long line of visitors, only twenty or so were friends of the late George Pellew. The rest were strangers, brought in to muddle the picture. All were presented without a clue as to name or background. Yet G.P. had effortlessly sorted through this parade, greeting all his old friends by name except one, a girl who was now eighteen and had been only ten when he met her. She had changed, G.P. told her finally, adding rather rudely that he wondered if she still played the violin as badly as she had as a child. As Hodgson reported, not once in the years between 1892 and 1897 did "G.P." ever confuse a stranger for a friend of George Pellew—or vice versa. (Blum, *Ghost Hunters*)

"It was in September, 1932, that I first heard of Bobbie," writes Charles Drayton Thomas in his book *An Amazing Experiment*. "A letter came from [the town of] Nelson, in Lancashire, asking if I would attempt to obtain information from a boy of ten who had recently died from diphtheria." His correspondent, a Mr. Hatch, provided the bare minimum of information, writing:

> For ten years my stepdaughter has lived with me and my wife, and her little boy has been the life and centre of our lives. He was particularly intelligent and extraordinarily loving and lovable. A few weeks ago he died suddenly of diphtheria, aged 10. The loss is so dreadful that we feel we must ask if you can in any way obtain comfort similar to that recounted in your book, *Life Beyond Death*.
>
> We feel that the very strong love and comradeship we had should make communication possible, if it is ever possible. I confess that my education (I have an honours degree in science) makes my faith in such matters very halting.

For some years, Thomas had been working with the British medium Gladys Osborne Leonard. He determined to present the letter to her, not by letting her read it, but simply by placing it in her hand after telling her, "I have a very earnest request for news of a little boy Bobbie." He writes, "Needless to say I had folded [the letter] in such a way that no information could be ascertained by glancing at it. Added to this I watched carefully during the few minutes it was in the medium's hands, and observed that her eyes did not open."

In the ensuing dialogue, Mrs. Leonard, speaking through a spirit control named Feda, asked if Bobbie was "connected with a town, not London but a town, not one of the biggest in the provinces? ... It is a busy place, but not one of the very biggest of those towns. I don't think you would call it the biggest of those towns, and yet it is a largish place where they are concentrating on important things ... Do you know if some manufacturing places are on the banks of a canal or river there? It does not feel pretty enough to call a river because of the buildings and the things on the side of it ... Oh, are they partly making some stuff, there in this place, is it earthenware or pottery, something like stone?"

This was all correct, and mostly unknown to Thomas. Mr. Hatch, informed by mail of the sitting, observed, "Bobbie had a great friend who is a working man engaged usually in making mortar and cement." Nevertheless, the cautious Mr. Hatch was not especially won over by this first sitting: "If Bobbie were trying to communicate I cannot believe that he would refer to any of the matters mentioned ... I have heard it said that those who are desperately anxious for evidence are very credulous. I do not think it is so with me. My fear is lest I should be deceived by evidence that can be explained by some other faculty of the mind, perhaps one that has not been investigated as yet."

In later sessions, Mrs. Leonard came through with a great deal of additional information. Only excerpts can be provided here. She saw "a photograph of Bobbie in a rather peculiar position? I see him full faced, or very nearly full faced, but with something in front of him, as if there is a board in front of him." This referred to the last photo ever taken of Bobbie, in which he was dressed as the Jack of Hearts, wearing a sandwich board. "Will you ask also if he had been given—think it must have been a joke—something new that he was fond of using or wearing on his head, something round; if it was a cap it had no peak to it." Part of the costume was a crown in the form of a pack of cards. "And did he use something made of celluloid, something that he used and they wanted him to stop using it? They thought it might make a flame or explosion." Bobbie had purchased a used "cinematograph lantern," and his family members were worried about the highly inflammable celluloid film.

It was established, through the séances, that Bobbie practiced boxing in the attic. In January, 1933, Mr. Hatch mailed a question to the medium: "What did he do in the attic besides boxing?"

Feda, the spirit control, answered,

> What are you showing me? Did you pull a string out of the wall? Bobbie did some funny things for a boy, now look, he is going to the wall and he seems as if he is untwisting something and he is pulling something from the wall, either thick string or rope, and on the end he seems to be fixing something carefully. That is important, what he is doing with it. It is the pulling it out that seems to be the important thing. It is something about drawing it out as far as is possible and then letting it go back to the wall again. It is something that he seemed to do rather regularly.

Mr. Hatch confirmed that "in the attic he had among other things, an arrangement for strengthening the muscles ... Drawing it out was the important thing, and he did it rather regularly."

The online *Psi Encyclopedia* of the Society for Psychical Research observes,

> In eleven sittings, a large number of statements were made about Bobbie and the manner of his death. Of these, 100 were specific and correct with regard to the actual circumstances: for example, the Jack of Hearts fancy dress costume he had once worn, gymnastic exercises he practised and the equipment he used. Thirty-eight more general statements were vaguely relevant, and 26 were poor. Only seven were actually wrong.

The most important and evidential material concerned the cause of Bobbie's death, which, according to the communicators on the other side, was more than simply diphtheria. Thomas reports being told, "There had been something which previously weakened his constitution so that when diphtheria attacked him he could not withstand it ... This predisposition might be traced to something which happened nine weeks before the boy's death."

Questioned on this point, Feda said: "Pipes—pipes, he just says this—pipes. That word should be sufficient." Thomas writes,

This seemed to suggest infection from defective drainage, and I expected that the family would acquiesce in this. But they refused to accept any suggestion of the kind, and replied that they could not trace the matter at all, that the word "pipes" conveyed nothing to them, and that they did not know of any event nine weeks before the boy's death which could in any sense be thought to connect with it ...

Persevering effort ... finally brought to light something which the family had not known, namely, that in a remote spot, where Bobbie had frequently played during the weeks preceding his death, water issued through pipes from springs in the hillside.

It was eventually ascertained by professional analysis that although the spring water is pure, yet the pools into which it falls are badly contaminated ...

The whole story centres round the fact that Bobbie and a boy friend had formed themselves into a secret society which they called "the Gang," and in the early summer began to frequent a place called "The Heights" for play and adventure. Being a secret society, they did not divulge the whereabouts of their playing-ground.

Thomas points out that

no suggestion of infection from contaminated water had occurred to anyone until it was hinted in these messages; and further, it was entirely due to information given in these trance conversations that we

> learnt that Bobbie had played by these pools. Six months elapsed before their existence was discovered, and meanwhile the communicators at almost every sitting were giving clue after clue, thus leading us finally to the spot where the pipes and contaminated pools were found.

How are we to understand all this? Make sense of it? Put it into a context we can grasp? Without a context, any one of these cases is no more than a ghost story. It may be creepy or diverting, but it's not part of any larger world-picture.

The purpose of this book is to suggest a few such world-pictures, which I call models. None of these models is intended to be a complete representation of reality. Actually, no model can fully reproduce reality; the map is not the territory, the menu is not the meal. And these four models no doubt all have weaknesses, gaps, and gray areas. But I've found them useful in considering this subject, and I hope you will, too.

Now for brief detour into autobiography. It seems pretty standard for people who write books like this to say that they started out as complete skeptics and found their minds changed by the evidence. This is more or less true for me, but with one difference.

When I was seventeen, I went through a summer of soul-seeking in which I investigated various spiritual and religious options, including Christianity. Basically, I was looking for something to believe in. At one point, reading a book about Christianity, I came across a passage that advised me to engage in what I would now call a guided meditation. With eyes shut, I imagined myself approaching a closed door. The door opened, and behind it was the figure of Jesus Christ welcoming me.

The upshot of this meditation was truly surprising to me. I experienced an overwhelming sense of peace and light—specifically a reddish-orange glow that suffused everything around me. I saw that my fellow human beings were essentially spirits temporarily housed in physical vessels, and that the whole world had only a tenuous and fleeting reality. There was nothing to worry about, nothing to fear.

This sense of "the peace that passes understanding" stayed with me for a couple of days. It was as though I were moving through a dream. I remember riding on the train to my summer job in New York City and visualizing all the people around me as spirit forms rather than flesh and blood. I don't mean I was actually seeing them as ghosts, only that I felt deeply that their true reality was spiritual and not physical. I even remember that at one point, crossing a busy Manhattan street, I had a close shave with a speeding car, yet I felt complete unconcern. It didn't matter to me if I got hit or even killed, because this was all barely more than a dream anyway.

Predictably, the feeling faded. What is perhaps more surprising is that I largely forgot about it. I simply brushed it aside, figured it meant nothing, and eventually embraced atheism and humanism as my belief system. You might wonder how I could brush off such a powerful experience. I'll have something to say about that in Chapter One.

In any case, I remained a complete skeptic about all things paranormal, spiritual, and religious for twenty years. I was thirty-seven when this began to change. I must have been going through something like an early midlife crisis, because in the first six months of that year I moved three times to three different cities. Meanwhile, I was writing a novel, *Comes the Dark*, which dealt with esoteric themes far from my usual subject matter. And although my career was going well and I had no obvious cause for complaint, I found myself deeply dissatisfied. I kept asking myself: Is this all there is?

Though it sounds ridiculous, I kept coming back to a bit of business from an episode of *The Simpsons*. When all the power in Springfield goes out, an assembly line contraption that belches out fake vomit is brought to a standstill, and all the workers moan. Later, power is restored, the machine kicks into life again, and the workers cheer. I felt this was a metaphor for my life. Here I was, belching out paperback books one after another on a kind of assembly line, cheering a little when each one hit the stores, and yet what did it all mean? How was it any more significant than cranking out novelty vomit or any other triviality? *Doh!*

With these (perhaps weird) thoughts haunting me, I began to look into the paranormal in a serious way for the first time. Before this, the only things I'd read about paranormal phenomena were books by skeptics like James Randi and Martin Gardner or dismissive asides by rationalists like Isaac Asimov and Carl Sagan. I had no firsthand acquaintance with the literature and in fact was curiously repelled by it. I remember one time a friend of mine, for a laugh, insisted we go into a paranormal bookstore, and while he enjoyed making fun of the inventory, I felt deeply uncomfortable and just wanted to get out. Something about the paranormal unnerved me and made me keep my distance. It took me some time to cautiously explore the more respectable margins of the field before wading in to deeper waters.

Eventually, I began to see that phenomena such as telepathy, clairvoyance (today more often known as remote viewing), precognition, and psychokinesis were supported by substantial evidence. But I was still unsold on the idea of life after death.

What began to change my mind, oddly enough, was the TV show *Crossing Over*, featuring medium John Edward. The show was a surprise hit, and I watched an episode merely out of curiosity, expecting to find it ridiculous. I already knew about mentalist tricks like cold reading, and I figured Edward was just pulling a fast one. In many ways this assumption was easy to support; his fast-talking style, reminiscent of a used-car salesman trying to close the deal, did not necessarily inspire confidence. And there was no way of knowing how much information he or his staff might have gathered about the people in the audience.

Still, some of his hits were intriguing. I began to watch the show regularly and even took notes on it. I also investigated skeptical websites looking for a convincing explanation of the more dramatic hits. For the most part, I was disappointed. Either no explanation was offered for the best hits, or the explanation was hopelessly inadequate. One example that sticks in my memory was a reading for an audience member named Catherine, whose husband had died some time earlier. Here's part of the transcript:

John: Why is Niagara Falls significant?

Catherine: We was just there.

John: You were just at Niagara Falls, ok.

Catherine: Me and my daughter.

John: Did you find a feather there?

Catherine: Yes, and my daughter ...

John: Did you tell your daughter that was from daddy?

Catherine: Yes.

John: Ok, this is a validation that he was there for you, ok? 'Cause he's showing me the feather. Lucky for you that's my mother's symbol when she communicates with me. I find feathers. So it was a very easy symbol for me to get. But I need to validate for you that it was definitely, definitely him there for her.

Catherine: Thank you.

So Edward told Catherine that he was getting "Niagara Falls," and in fact she had just been there. He asked if she'd found a feather there, and the woman said yes. He asked if she'd told her daughter that the feather was "from daddy." Catherine confirmed this, too.

I found this hit pretty evidential, although I recognized that non-paranormal explanations were possible. Maybe Catherine blogged about her experience, and Edward's showrunners researched her social media history. Maybe she talked about the feather while waiting for the show to start, and eavesdroppers planted among the audience members relayed the info to their boss.

These explanations struck me as unlikely. Social media

was less pervasive in 2001 than it is today, and if Edward had flunkies performing these tasks, inevitably one or more of them would have signed lucrative tell-all deals with tabloid news outlets.

Looking for a better answer, I found a website called *Skeptic Report*, which covered the reading in the article "Birds of a Feather," by Claus Larsen. *Skeptic Report* had it all figured out.

First they took issue with the fact that Catherine said "and my daughter ..." just before Edward said, "Did you tell your daughter that [i.e., the feather] was from daddy?" According to the article, the words *my daughter* would have clued in Edward to the feather's claimed significance.

But would it? The mere fact that Catherine said "and my daughter ..." would not lead anyone to infer that Catherine told her daughter that the feather "was from daddy." Moreover, when I watched a rerun of the show, I found crosstalk at this very point. Edward said, "Did you tell your daughter ..." at the same moment when Catherine was saying, "... and my daughter." Rather than reacting to her statement, he was talking over it and partly drowning it out.

How about the feather itself? *Skeptic Report* is unimpressed, informing us:

> According to the 35th Annual Niagara Falls Christmas Bird Count on Saturday, December 29th, 2001, a total of 101 species of birds were found, and a total of 49,744 birds in Niagara Falls, NY.
>
> There are also quite a few photos on the web from Niagara Falls with birds in them:

> [Links to bird photos are provided.]
>
> Tons of birds on these ones.
>
> I think we can safely say that it would not be uncommon to find a feather at Niagara Falls.

No doubt there are lots of birds at Niagara Falls. There are lots of birds everywhere. But although I've been around birds every day of my life, I've seldom noticed feathers on the ground, and to the best of my recollection I've never seen a kid pick up a feather. Moreover, I've never heard anyone tell a child that a feather was a gift from a deceased parent.

The whole "explanation" is an obvious example of rationalizing after the fact. If Edward had said that Catherine's husband was run over by a dump truck in Newark, *Skeptic Report* would cite statistics and photos proving there are many dump trucks in Newark. When you think of Newark, aren't dump trucks the first thing that come to mind? And since people sometimes get run over by dump trucks, it was easy for Edward to guess that the husband had died this way. Why, it's just common sense!

Except it isn't.

As I searched for other skeptical accounts of Edward's readings, I encountered many debunking exercises just as unconvincing as this one. Gradually it dawned on me that *any* hits Edward obtained could be rationalized away by a determined doubter. This made me skeptical of the skeptics and a bit more willing to take people like John Edward seriously.

At any rate, *Crossing Over* broke down some of my resistance to the idea of mediumship and life after death. I still wasn't convinced, but I was at least willing to investigate. I started reading up on historical case histories and discovered that in the heyday of scientific exploration of mediumship, from the late nineteenth century until roughly the 1930s, there were mediums who were extensively tested with every possible precaution against fraud, and yet who continued to produce strikingly accurate results. These included Leonora Piper, Gladys Osborne Leonard, and Eileen Garrett—not coincidentally, the three mediums featured in the cases at the beginning of this introduction.

The fact that this research took place a century ago, more or less, did not particularly bother me, since the cases were so well documented and since the investigators struck me as intelligent, diligent, and honest. Still, if no comparable evidence had been available from more recent times, I would have been less convinced. But although the scientific examination of mediumship fell somewhat out of favor in the middle of the twentieth century—primarily owing to the influence of J.B. Rhine, who shifted parapsychology toward statistical testing of ESP—there are some modern cases that are just as dramatic as the old ones.

For instance, the murder of Jacqui Poole.

Jacqueline Poole was a twenty-five-year-old part-time barmaid who lived in the West London suburb of Ruislip. On February 13, 1983, her dead body was found in her apartment by her boyfriend's father. She had been raped, beaten, and strangled two days earlier.

The next day, Monday, a young woman named Christine Holohan, who was studying to become a professional medium, learned about the murder from some friends. That night, she had a disturbing vision of a woman calling herself "Jacqui Hunt," not Jacqui Poole. Although the information had not been made public at the time, it later developed that Hunt was Jacqui Poole's maiden name.

On Tuesday evening Holohan experienced a second contact with Jacqui Poole, whom she perceived as the "white outline of a person ... [a] white energy of light ... [and] a clear voice" in her ear.

In their authoritative article "A Possibly Unique Case of Psychic Detection," Guy Lyon Playfair and Montague Keen relate what Jacqui Poole told Holohan:

> Poole had been supposed to go to work on the night of the murder, two men having called for her, but she decided not to go as she was not feeling well. She had then a visit from a man she knew, a friend of a friend whom she had never liked. She let him in, thinking he might have a message from her boyfriend.

Having been given this information, which later proved to be correct, Holohan went to the police, meeting with Patrolman Tony Batters and Detective Constable Andrew Smith. Batters' detailed notes indicate that she provided 130 separate items of information about the crime. Her only apparent error was in placing the murder on "late Saturday night," when it actually occurred on Friday night. Interestingly, the date of the murder was one of the few pieces of information that would have been available in the media.

Playfair and Keen list many of Holohan's specific statements as recorded by Tony Batters in his notebook.

"She was attacked in the bathroom." Probably correct. Though the body was found in another room, a damaged bathroom towel rack and disarranged bathroom rug suggested that the attack commenced there.

"There was an envelope and a letter. Just come. A black address book ... Furniture was rearranged. Settee cushions moved. Out of place ... I changed my clothes twice, she says." Correct. The police officers had discovered a recently delivered letter at the apartment, along with the address book. The settee cushions had been thrown on the floor. And Jacqui Poole had changed clothes twice that day.

"Two cups in kitchen. One washed up. She made a cup of coffee." Also correct. Only two cups had been left out in the otherwise tidy kitchen. One had been washed; the other was half full of coffee.

Holohan said Jacqui Poole had traveled in criminal circles but had recently decided to turn her life around. A friend later described a conversation with Poole shortly before her murder in which she expressed these sentiments.

The medium said Poole had suffered from depression and was taking prescription pills for it. Correct. She said Poole was in the middle of a divorce. Correct, but this fact had been published in the press.

The murderer, she said, was connected with the ex-husband. "The link is with nick. Both had the same friend who was in nick. Not nick, she says, 'bird.' She went to visit him two weeks before."

Nick is British slang for a police station or prison, while *bird* is slang for a detention center. Holohan "did not understand the difference," Batters noted in later comments on his own notes. But Jacqui Poole evidently did know the difference and was at pains to amend the message.

The statement about Poole's last visit to the "nick" was correct; she had been there exactly two weeks before her body was found.

Holohan did not give the murderer's name, but she described him: "Five foot eightish ... Dark skin, coloured, Afro-wavy hair. Early 20s. She knows him. April-May birthday. He's Taurus. Tattoos on his arms. Swords? Snake? Rose? I get a name, Tony. He has a nickname, not a proper name."

The man eventually convicted of the crime was Anthony Ruark, of mixed-race origins, 5'9", born in April, twenty-three years old in 1983, with many tattoos.

Pressed for the nickname, Holohan went into a light trance and, via automatic writing, produced the word *pokie*. Ruark's nickname was Pokie.

She told police: "He's been working recently, like painting or decorating. Doesn't have a regular job, not a proper job. He's cool, sly, got into places before. And he's clever with cars. Grease monkey, she calls it."

All of this was correct. Ruark's only legitimate occupation was that of plasterer, and he had worked at that job on one or two days during the week before the murder. Otherwise, he made his money through burglary and auto theft. He was known as a good mechanic.

"He's got a girlfriend. She knew Jacqui. She's dark-haired, small, pretty. Got a C in her initials." Batters later confirmed that Ruark's girlfriend was a "petite and good-looking brunette whose surname begins with C," and that Poole knew her.

All of the names Holohan mentioned—Betty, Sylvia, Terry, Tony, Barbara Stone—were connected to the victim. Betty was Poole's mother. Sylvia was the mother of Poole's boyfriend. Terry was Poole's brother. Tony was the murderer, Anthony Ruark. The name Barbara Stone remained unexplained until years later when it was learned that she was a close friend of Poole who died in an auto accident about two years before the murder.

Holohan also mentioned someone who lived in "a flat over a newspaper shop." This turned out to be Poole's best friend, a woman named Gloria, who lived in just such an apartment.

Asked to determine the location of jewelry stolen from Jacqui's flat, Holohan used automatic writing and produced the words *Ickeham* and *garden* and the number 221. Ickeham was understood as an attempt to write Ickenham, a suburb located between the murder scene and Ruark's home. Years later, Batters followed up on this clue with interesting, though inconclusive, results. He discovered that there was only one street in Ickenham where the numbers went as high as 221—Swakeleys Road. However, where there should have been a 221, there was an unmarked public garden. Under some rocks he discovered a six-inch by seven-inch hole, now empty.

Playfair and Keen write:

> It is of course possible that the hole was made after 1983, perhaps by children playing, yet it must be granted that it is quite a coincidence to find an ideal hiding place for a handful of rings and bracelets at

> what may well once have been the garden of No. 221 on the only road in the area in question with that many house numbers.

Batters reckoned that the location was directly on the path Ruark took when he left the murder scene in Ruislip and returned home.

Even after all this, there was no solid evidence against Ruark or anyone else in 1983, and the case remained unsolved for more than sixteen years. Eventually, advances in DNA technology made it possible to more thoroughly examine the physical evidence connected to the case. A DNA match was sufficient to convict Ruark.

Playfair and Keen sum up:

> As Batters has repeatedly told us, the only possible single source for all the information [provided by Holohan] is Jacqueline Poole ... Tony Batters stated that "I've accepted the fact that Jacqui communicated with Christine," as, he has told us, have all his police colleagues with whom he has discussed the case.

The end result of all this was that I became increasingly persuaded that the idea of life after death was not crazy, after all. I even started blogging about it. Over a period of twenty years, I've turned out more than 1600 blog posts, the majority of which concern evidence for psi (ESP and PK) and the afterlife. I've had many interesting interactions online with my readers, who've helped me to shape and develop my ideas, often by putting forward a more skeptical point of view that has required me to reconsider or further develop my own opinion. As of this writing, the blog is closing in on 50,000 comments, so as you can see, I've had a lot of feedback.

One issue that I keep coming back to in the blog is the one I broached a few pages ago. How can we understand these anomalous phenomena and put them in some kind of intellectual framework that makes sense? Not necessarily to explain the mechanism by which they operate, though perhaps our speculations can bring us a little closer to such an understanding, but to find a way to integrate these seemingly inexplicable events into our picture of the world.

A century ago, psychical researcher Richard Hodgson recalled some conversations with a friend on the subject of life after death. His friend maintained that an afterlife "was not only incredible, but inconceivable," while Hodgson thought "it was at least conceivable." (Myers, *Human Personality*)

The person with whom Hodgson was speaking had died by the time he wrote down this reminiscence. He was, in fact, none other than George Pellew, whom we met in the account of Leonora Piper's sittings. If we are to credit Mrs. Piper's mediumship, then Pellew, once deceased, no longer found an afterlife either inconceivable or incredible. On the contrary, he found it "clear as daylight."

Dying is apparently one way to resolve all doubts. But short of that rather drastic step, perhaps we can *partially* resolve our doubts by making the afterlife, if not less incredible, then at least more conceivable. That's the idea behind this book.

CHAPTER ONE: THE FIRST MODEL

A fully immersive first-person virtual-reality game

YOU PROBABLY REMEMBER my mystical experience as a seventeen-year-old, which lasted for a couple of days. But remembering it was more than I was able to do, at least for a long time. I somehow suppressed a memory of what you might think would be a life-changing episode.

Weird, huh? But here's the thing. I've found it's remarkably easy to forget anomalous events. From experience, I know that unless I immediately write down a striking psi experience—say, a confirmed premonition or an amazing synchronicity—I will be unable to recall it even thirty minutes later. It vanishes like the memory of a dream. I've also noticed that it's all too easy to forget case histories of, say, experiments with mediums that really ought to be memorable. I'll spend a good deal of time summarizing a case for a blog post, and a few weeks later, it's largely slipped my mind.

Am I plagued by a bad memory? I don't think so, because it's not just me. In fact, this problem is astonishingly common.

Sittings with Eusapia Palladino, by Everard Feilding, documents a series of séances with a controversial Italian medium. The book includes journal entries by the researchers, a highly experienced team who, among them, had successfully debunked more than one hundred mediums of Palladino's type—so-called physical mediums, who, in darkness or dim light, apparently caused objects to move, breezes to blow, and musical instruments to play. Palladino was known to cheat—she even bragged about it—so the researchers no doubt thought it would be easy to add her to their list of fakes. They found, however, that if they took the trouble to secure Palladino in such a way that cheating was impossible, a variety of dramatic phenomena still took place. For the first time they found themselves confronted by séances they could not explain.

Even when Palladino's hands, feet, and knees were securely held, the table at which they sat would levitate, sometimes remaining aloft for a full minute. In an attempt to force down the table, one or two men would climb onto it, but it would remain suspended in air, bobbing like a raft, even as another man crawled underneath with a lamp to guard against fraud. More than once, Palladino, still in her chair, was levitated onto the table and, once, even above the tabletop, as the researchers passed their hands between the surface of the table and the legs of the hovering chair. Items of furniture moved freely around the room at a long distance from the medium, and one small table sometimes climbed atop a larger one. Inside a curtained-off area called a cabinet, musical instruments—a banjo, music box, bell, tambourine, and guitar, among others—would play by themselves, occasionally emerging from the cabinet to play in different parts of the room. Invisible hands would clutch the researchers even when Palladino's own hands were restrained.

In their journals, the researchers reported their frustration and confusion, but also a more interesting fact—that after a day or two, the most dramatic and persuasive effects produced by Palladino had somehow vanished from their memory. When reviewing contemporaneous notes taken during each session, they were often surprised to discover how many astonishing feats Palladino performed just a couple of days earlier.

With regard to one of the first sittings, Feilding notes:

> My mind was not prepared to accept the phenomena which occurred, and yet I was unable to suggest any loophole for fraud in the production of any of them ... We were still fresh at the game, still alertly suspicious of every movement of Eusapia; somewhat annoyed, to speak frankly, at our failure to detect any fraud at the first séance, and determined to get even with her. We tied her feet, and then presently forgot that we had tied them, and ... did not even remember it the next day.

Of the third sitting, Feilding writes:

> On reading through, last night, the translation of the shorthand notes of the third séance, we [i.e., Feilding and colleague Herewood Carrington] were both surprised to find what an entirely different impression we had retained of what had taken place from that which we derived from the notes. All the more remarkable manifestations had receded in our memory ... and if, before reading the notes, we had been asked to give an account of the séance, we should certainly have said that it had been almost barren of results ...

> During the third séance, [the table] remained motionless for long periods together, and the impression upon our minds was that the use of [a device to secure the table] had floored the medium. The notes, however, show that several complete levitations did, in point of fact, take place ... We had completely forgotten a great portion of [various other phenomena] until we read the notes.

In a supplementary comment written later, Feilding says that his original, early notes

> exist as a record of our critical, indeed hostile state of mind. The first two séances had in fact left no enduring mark upon us. They had astonished us, puzzled us, vexed us ... The ordinary effect of the sudden confrontation of a fairly balanced mind with a merely bizarre fact is a reaction: the mind rejects it, refuses to consider it. And the more bizarre the fact, the stronger the reaction ... Tables, we knew, or thought we knew, do not go into the air by themselves; curtains do not bulge out without some mechanical agency; and although we saw them do so, we still refused to believe that they did.

In his memoir *Travels*, Michael Crichton includes an account of a so-called PK (psychokinesis) party in which guests tried bending spoons and other pieces of metal by the power of the mind. Naturally, Crichton was skeptical, as was his friend, Anne-Marie.

> Rubbing her spoon, Anne-Marie said, "I don't think this is going to work. This is silly. I just don't see how it can work."
>
> I looked down at her hands. Her spoon was bending.
>
> "Look, Anne-Marie ..."
>
> Anne-Marie laughed. Her spoon was like rubber. She easily twisted the spoon into knots.

Crichton thought his own spoon would never bend, until another friend said, "Congratulations."

> I looked down. My spoon had begun to bend. I hadn't even realized. The metal was completely pliable, like soft plastic.

After bending the bowl of the spoon in half with minimal pressure, Crichton chose a fork, which "twisted like a pretzel." He did this with a few more items. After which, something even more remarkable happened.

> I got bored. I didn't do any more spoon bending. I went and got coffee and a cookie. I was now far more interested in what kind of cookies they had for me than anything else.

His interest did not return. "The room was full of people doing the same thing, and it seemed very ordinary. Kind of boring." He adds that "this sense of boredom often seems to accompany 'psychic' phenomena. At first the event appears exciting and mysterious, but very quickly it becomes so mundane that it can no longer hold your interest."

Then there is the curious case of Miss Z. This young lady was the subject of experiments conducted by parapsychologist Charles Tart in the early 1960s. The test subject, known in the literature as Miss Z to protect her privacy, said she often had out-of-body experiences (or OBEs) while asleep. To test this claim, she agreed to sleep in Tart's laboratory, hooked up to EEG monitors. The EEG results were highly unusual; in *The End of Materialism*, Tart writes that "one of the world's leading authorities on sleep research, psychiatrist William Dement, ... agreed with me that it was a distinctive pattern, but we had no idea what it meant." More interesting, though, was that Miss Z correctly identified a target number hidden in the room, which she had seen while out of the body. Although there is a very small chance that she could have seen the number's (exceedingly dim) reflection in a wall clock, she could not have seen the target directly from her bed, nor could she have gotten out of bed without unhooking the monitors; moreover, the period of her reported OBE corresponds to the unusual EEG activity. Odds against simply guessing the number are 100,000 to 1.

This seems like a potentially breakthrough case, and we would expect Tart to have continued the experiments and replicated the results, while eliminating any possible source of information leakage, such as the faint reflection. But that's not what happened. Instead, Miss Z relocated to another city, and Tart let the experiments lapse, even though, as he notes,

"People who can have an OBE on demand are, to put it mildly, rare."

Looking back, he says he finds his decision not to follow through somewhat peculiar. He notes the "long history of parapsychological experiments where powerful results were obtained in the beginning, investigators got excited, and then the results petered out for no apparent reason or the experimenter got involved in other things ... Sometimes it makes you wonder: Are we being led? Baited? Intellectually teased?"

People forget striking events they ought to remember; they lose interest just as things are getting interesting; they don't follow up on groundbreaking experiments that could shift everyone's perception. Why? What's going on here?

As long as we're asking questions, let's ask a few more:

• Why do we react in a panic to the very idea of experimenting with mind-altering chemicals, even throwing people in jail for doing so?

• Why do we pass laws penalizing psychics and mediums, or uphold religious injunctions against dabbling in the occult?

• Why do some intellectuals spend their lives, or at least much of their free time, combatting any suggestion that the paranormal has some validity?

• Why do so many people say they're never really convinced, no matter how much evidence they see?

• Why do researchers who choose to study the paranormal find themselves ostracized, their careers sidetracked, their reputations maligned?

• Why do we reflexively dismiss and ridicule those who claim to be in touch with higher levels of consciousness?

Some people, seeing the marginalization of the paranormal, say the government or a secret cabal is behind it all. I don't think so. Governments and cabals are notoriously inept.

George Hansen, author of *The Trickster and the Paranormal*, offers a more sophisticated take. He argues at length for the liminality (marginal nature) of psi. He points to the marginal status of shamans, medicine women, necromancers, and ghost hunters in most societies—including ours, which relegates the paranormal to horror stories, humor, and "woo." This socially mandated liminality keeps us from accepting the paranormal or even taking it seriously.

This is probably true. But what is the nature of Hansen's "liminality" and why does it seem to function as a built-in feature of the universe? One answer is that it actually *is* a built-in feature of the universe, a feature that helps to ensure our continued full immersion in our perceived reality by marginalizing anyone who starts to see "behind the veil," and by sequestering and scrubbing our own memories before they can be preserved long-term. It's equivalent to the steps taken in *The Matrix* to keep everybody believing in the shared illusion.

If you look at it this way, doubts and even denial in the face of intellectually convincing evidence may support the idea that our reality, the cosmos itself, is a kind of virtual-reality simulation—not literally, in the sense of being a rendered environment produced by algorithms on a laptop, but conceptually, in the sense that it is only an appearance and not the true underlying reality. It is Plato's cave, in which the shadows of things on the wall are mistaken for the things themselves.

Moreover, this simulation is designed to be *fully immersive*, an experiential environment that envelops us completely and absorbs our full attention. To the extent that we become aware of nonphysical existence, we are less than fully immersed in this environment, and that's not how the game is played.

In short, the world works this way *because that's how it's set up to work.* We are biologically hardwired and socially conditioned to pay no attention to the man behind the curtain. If we notice him anyway, we are inclined to forget. If, despite everything, we remember, then we risk our own social, professional, and intellectual banishment (a prospect that gives us an additional incentive to forget).

I forget my little moments of psychic intuition—or my teenaged self's glimpse of a higher reality—because they threaten my full immersion in the role-playing game of my physical life. The researchers studying Eusapia Palladino forgot the most compelling moments of the séances for the same reason. Michael Crichton suddenly found spoon-bending boring, with the result that he didn't pursue it. What Charles Tart calls being baited, led, and teased might be understood as a veil of ignorance imposed by the conditions of our incarnation itself.

Well, maybe. But if this were the only reason for picturing our cosmos as a fully immersive virtual-reality environment, it would not be very persuasive. Some form of purely psychological or sociological analysis would serve equally well. Is there any reason to think this model is more than an intriguing daydream?

I think there is, and it's found in both parapsychology and mainstream science.

Anyone who's studied the evidence for survival that has accumulated in the 138 years since the founding of the Society for Psychical Research knows that a basic picture has emerged. This picture is incomplete and contains some contradictions, which we'll get to later. But in essence it goes like this:

Each of us is, as the popular saying goes, "a spiritual being having a physical experience." The body and brain are used by consciousness to navigate the physical world. At death, the spiritual consciousness is liberated from this vessel and undergoes an out-of-body experience. The OBE typically begins in familiar surroundings but can move quickly into a transitional zone, sometimes visualized as a tunnel or as a void. Passage through this zone brings the spirit into another plane of existence, where all memories of the now-concluded lifetime are relived in rapid succession, with startling clarity. Insights gleaned from this "life review" help the spirit to understand where he or she chose the wrong path or failed to live up to his or her potential.

After a period of recuperation, the refreshed spirit, inhabiting a spiritual body similar to that of the earthly incarnation, is introduced to an earthlike environment where the next phase of postmortem existence will play out. This environment is an idealized re-creation of earthly habitats, and is understood to be the product of the collective unconscious of all the spirits making use of it. A multiplicity of such environments exists, ranging from paradise conditions to nightmarish hells, each corresponding to the overall level of spiritual development of its inhabitants. Because spirits of similar developmental levels cluster together, and because their environment is made up out of their expectations and memories, people will tend to experience what they want and expect to experience.

In his book *90 Minutes in Heaven*, Don Piper, a born-again Christian, describes a near-death experience in which he found himself in a quintessentially Christian heaven, complete with "pearlescent gates," streets of gold, and choirs of angels. He came back convinced that he had been to heaven, though he remained skeptical of other NDEs that encompassed different, non-biblical experiences. He was sure that only his version of the afterlife could be real. But there's no reason to think it was any more or less real than any other experience, including the experiences of Hindus who often report being escorted to the afterlife by angelic messengers known as *yamdoots*, as recounted by Erlendur Haraldsson and Karlis Osis in *At the Hour of Death.*

Nineteenth-century spiritualist literature abounds in descriptions of the Summerland, a serene and beautiful environment enjoyed by most people after death. Gardens, cottages, and other homely delights are recounted in detail. People are said to create art, tend flowers, hold jobs, conduct research, and even—occasionally—partake of whiskey, cigars, and sex! Naturally, skeptics have had a field day with these accounts, but if the experience is a product of memory and expectation, then any earthly experience can be re-created with apparent reality. Yes, even whiskeys, cigars, and sex.

All such environments are temporary, serving as way stations that offer opportunities for learning and growth; eventually all spirits will move on, whether from paradise, hell, or one of the myriad spiritual planes in between. In the channeled book *The Road to Immortality*, the spirit of early psychical researcher F.W.H. Myers warns that Summerland is a plane of illusion, which he compares to the land of the Lotus Eaters in Greek mythology. The Lotus Eaters kept themselves perpetually intoxicated, existing in a hallucinatory state. Myers, as transcribed by Geraldine Cummins via automatic writing, insists that however attractive Summerland may be to its inhabitants, it is not ultimately real, and when an individual spirit recognizes this fact, he will be elevated to a higher plane.

The above story has been put together out of many different lines of inquiry. NDEs and OBEs, mediumship and automatic writing, deathbed visions and the mystical experiences known as "cosmic consciousness"—all have contributed to the story, and for the most part tend to reinforce and supplement each other. There is as much coherence and unanimity among our various sources, dating back to the nineteenth century or even earlier, as we might expect from a couple of centuries of reports on a distant, inaccessible place—Timbuktu, perhaps.

Now let's step back and look at all this from the standpoint of our virtual-reality model.

Imagine yourself playing a computer game. When you complete one level, you're automatically transitioned to the next level. This new, higher level is similar to the previous one, but the rules are somewhat different, and you've acquired some powerful new capabilities. Your avatar (your on-screen persona) may look different. You must learn new skills or hone the skills you already learned.

For our purposes, this is not just any computer game, but a virtual-reality (VR) game—the sort of game where you wear a special headset that immerses you in a computer-generated world. Everything about you seems real; and it *is* real, but only in the sense that it is a real *image*, a real artificial construction. The underlying reality, which you don't see, is very different. It's a reality of ones and zeros, digital data, which are processed behind the scenes. The trees, mountains, and living bodies in your virtual environment have, as their underlying reality, a vast invisible sea of algorithms and binary code.

What happens if you take off your VR headset, or allow it to slip partly off? You are no longer immersed in the virtual world, no longer seduced by its imagery or caught up in its drama. You may say, as film critic Roger Ebert did shortly before he died, "This is all an elaborate hoax."

What's necessary to lift the headset is an altered state of consciousness. This can be achieved in many different ways.

Salvia divinorum is a psychoactive plant that is usually smoked or chewed. Known more commonly as salvia or just Sally, the plant is legal in some jurisdictions and has a long history of use in traditional societies. Here are excerpts from the experiences of various salvia users.

> I took a big hit of Salvia ... I slipped out of the 2d [= two-dimensional] plane and was hovering over

my body for a brief moment.

Next thing I know my vision is getting saturated, literally like Photoshop effects, and then when I move my head even slightly it's like everything is warping and stretching, like a graphical bug, with pixels not loading, stuff like that.

Everything gets depth and becomes pixels, the ground gets depth and becomes pixels and starts moving and carrying [me] around on the pixels, while moving [I try] to look in between the pixels into nothing, and [try] to feel in between them.

I couldn't see anything at all. It was a kaleidoscope so intricate that the pieces were not visible to the naked eye. It was as if a computer took all of its pixels and scrambled them into some random configuration.

My vision seemed to be consistent [*sic*] of pixels like a computer, and all I had to do was turn away ... Turn away and look at the real reality, but I just couldn't.

Everything I was seeing was made of individual, single color pixels, like a TV screen, but the colors weren't limited at all! And they didn't have a definite shape, either. They were all roughly oval. Sort of pill-shaped, but I got more of the impression that they were like plant cells, with thin layers of membrane around each one that kept it binded [*sic*] to the others on the proper sequence.

The last friend I smoked it with had no idea what he was in for ... Straight away he seemed distressed ... Apparently he thought himself an icon in a video game, and he was trapped between planes of reality.

It's like nothing exists and all is just ... like fake or something.

This is when I realize that all of reality and everything that I knew to be true was false.

Salvia unzipped myself in half and everyone around me morphed into laughing jokers, causing me to believe that the world had played a giant trick on me and that everything I knew was totally fake.

Suddenly everyone I'd ever known, all the places I'd been, my whole life, had been a lie. It had been just a game, a silly puppet show, and it meant nothing in comparison to the depths of existence beyond my life, way into the infinity of the universe ... All along my life has been this insane charade which God has now chosen to break down.

The only way I can explain it is that it's almost like there are entities that are part of our subconscious

> mind and the collective unconscious. They are "behind the scenes" in making our objective reality. They are always shifting things to make them seem real and authentic, almost like this reality is just a sinister joke, or some sort of game we all play.
>
> I was transported into another dimension where I FINALLY understood life and all of its concepts and a multicolored being came to me and presented himself and explained to me that all we are as humans are tiny pixels working our hardest to play out life for beings above us ... We are all tiny pieces to an indescribably large puzzle.
>
> Salvia is the only thing I've done that has so completely shattered my reality and forced me to reassess my entire life and the way I live it.
>
> My old vision of death as simple oblivion has been wiped away, and it's very difficult for me to imagine death as anything other than a new transformation into the conscious energy we were before birth and will return to again.

Many of these people suffered intense psychological aftereffects as they struggled with the sense of having glimpsed a deeper reality that makes our normal, everyday experience seem like a game, a puzzle, "a silly puppet show." One person said, "It will leave you doubting your existence for years afterwards."

Perhaps salvia has this effect on people because our mundane experience really *is* a game of sorts—shadows on the wall of Plato's cave, or icons on a screen. Perhaps the ancient Vedic texts are correct when they describe this world as Maya, a world of appearances that masquerades as the one and only reality, or when they speak of our lives as Lila, meaning play-acting. Beyond Maya there is Brahman, ultimate reality. But because the pull of Maya is so strong—because the game is immersive (and addictive)—you will probably find it hard to let go.

Sometime between the eighth and fourteenth centuries, Buddhist monks on the high plateau of Tibet worried about much the same thing. They authored a document known in the West as the *Tibetan Book of the Dead*. It delineates various stages of postmortem existence, known as bardos. As is often the case with religious writings, the book is highly formalized, with successive stages neatly ordered in groups of seven and said to last for a specific number of days. Leaving aside these elaborations, the gist of the narrative is a set of instructions on how to best handle the dying process. You are told to expect a series of visions, both positive and negative, which are generated by your own mind but perceived as objectively real. You will find yourself fully immersed in these thought-forms, which reflect your deepest expectations, fears, and hopes, all the while cut off from your higher self. Only by realizing that the scenes before you are nothing more than a mental projection can you break free of the wheel of rebirth and avoid reincarnation. Most of us, not being spiritual adepts, can't manage it; we remain entangled in illusion and are eventually shuttled back to earth for a new lifetime.

Seeing past the illusions of the bardo is analogous to lifting the VR headset and emerging from the simulated reality that entraps you. Remaining caught up in illusion is akin to leaving the headset in place—which is so much easier.

Even in a typical postmortem experience, there are moments when the headset is lifted at least a little. Near-death experiencers commonly report an encounter with an intense light that contains or embodies all knowledge. They often equate the light with God. The *Tibetan Book of the Dead*, calling it "the clear light of being," identifies it as your own higher self. This is also a view put forward by prominent NDE researcher Kenneth Ring in his book *Life at Death*. However we understand the light, those who temporarily merged with it and then returned to life report that they were flooded with a complete knowledge of the universe.

Mystics report similar epiphanies. In 1901, Richard Maurice Bucke wrote an influential book titled *Cosmic Consciousness: A Study in the Evolution of the Human Mind*. The book is a compilation of accounts featuring persons both notable and unknown who underwent mystical experiences that uplifted their thought and character—essentially what psychologist Abraham Maslow called "peak experiences" and what Hindu tradition calls "kundalini experiences." My own reaction to the guided meditation about Jesus may possibly qualify as a case of this sort, at least to a certain extent.

Many of Bucke's best accounts were provided by his contemporaries—ordinary people whose lives were changed by a transcendent sense of oneness with the cosmos lasting anywhere from a few minutes to a few days. One such case involves a woman identified only as C.M.C.

After a lifelong search for spiritual meaning, C.M.C. experienced "the supreme event of my life ... the outcome of those years of passionate search." Worn out by "the pain and tension deep in the core and center of my being," she submitted to a higher power and let go of herself entirely. The result was "a feeling of perfect health" and a new appreciation of "how bright and beautiful [was] the day." She goes on:

> The sense of lightness and expansion kept increasing, the wrinkles smoothed out of everything, there was nothing in all the world that seemed out of place ... The light and color glowed, the atmosphere seemed to quiver and vibrate around and within me. Perfect rest and peace and joy were everywhere, and, more strange than all, there came to me a sense of some serene, magnetic presence—grand and all pervading ... I was seeing and comprehending the sublime meaning of things, the reasons for all that had before been hidden and dark ...
>
> I felt myself going, losing myself. Then I was terrified, but with a sweet terror. I was losing my consciousness, my identity, but was powerless to hold myself. Now came a period of rapture ... The Perfect Wisdom, truth, love and purity! And with the rapture came the insight. In that same wonderful moment of what might be called supernal bliss, came illumination. I saw with intense inward vision the

atoms or molecules, of which seemingly the universe is composed—I know not whether material or spiritual—rearranging themselves, as the cosmos (in its continuous, everlasting life) passes from *order to order*. What joy when I saw there was no break in the chain—not a link left out—everything in its place and time. Worlds, systems, all blended in one harmonious whole. Universal life, synonymous with universal love! ...

How long the vision lasted I cannot tell. In the morning I awoke with a slight headache, but with the spiritual sense so strong that what we call the actual, material things surrounding me seemed shadowy and unreal. My point of view was entirely changed. Old things had passed away and all had become new. The ideal had become real, the old *real* had lost its former reality and had become shadowy. This *shadowy unreality* of *external things* did not last many days. *Every longing of the heart was satisfied*, every question answered, the "pent-up, aching rivers" had reached the ocean—I loved infinitely and was infinitely loved! ...

Out of this experience was born an unfaltering trust. Deep in the soul, below pain, below all the distraction of life, is a silence vast and grand—an infinite ocean of calm, which nothing can disturb; Nature's own exceeding peace, which "passes understanding." (all emphases in original)

At the risk of interpreting a sublime experience in dispiritingly mundane terms, C.M.C.'s rapturous flood of knowledge could be described as a data dump. No longer focused on appearances, she was, in a sense, shown the source code behind the rendered images, the database that underlies the simulation. For some timeless interval she enjoyed direct, unfettered access to this source, and could see the whole pattern: the universal plan and order, the laws and constants, everything. She saw the components of the universe "rearranging themselves, as the cosmos ... passes from order to order," perhaps in a manner similar to the changes on a computer screen, where one ordered pattern is replaced by a new ordered pattern every time the screen refreshes. She peered behind the veil, saw through the illusions.

But it was only temporary. The headset slipped down again, and she was back in the familiar, rendered, virtual-reality world.

In the VR model, our perceived experience can vary from level to level in the game. Very rarely, we emerge from the game altogether. These brief escapes are peak experiences, mystical transports, episodes of cosmic consciousness, spiritual epiphanies. They form the basis for religions, philosophies, art, music, morals, culture. In these moments we—like Melville's Ahab—"strike through the mask" of our false reality, penetrating nearer to the heart of things.

But come on. How can mysticism tell us anything about reality? That's what science is for, isn't it? What we need is not metaphysics, but physics.

Okay, let's look at physics.

I begin this excursus with a *caveat lector* (reader beware):

I'm not a scientist and can only report what I've read in books and essays. Moreover, there are many differing interpretations of quantum physics, all of which are correct in terms of mathematics, but none of which has attained a consensus as the final, authoritative explanation of how things work. Victorian author A.W. Kinglake thought churches should have the words "Important if True" carved over their entryways. Perhaps this section of the book should have a similar heading.

In the scientific community, there is a small but vocal faction arguing that the space-time universe actually is grounded in pure information. The late physicist John Wheeler, who came around to this position, summarized it as "everything is information" or, more pithily, "it from bit."

Why would anybody think such a crazy thing? Much of it has to do with the oddities and paradoxes of the quantum (subatomic) realm. Experts have long known that a subatomic entity can behave like either a particle or a wave, which is not how objects in everyday life behave. In fact, it's not consistent with the behavior of objects as such. It's more consistent with the way information works.

The basis for particle-wave duality, also known as quantum indeterminacy, is the famed double-slit experiment, which has been repeated and confirmed countless times. Electrons beamed through a pair of slits will, if measured one way, produce an interference pattern consistent with a wave, but will, if measured another way, produce a scattershot pattern consistent with individual particles. The pattern on the screen depends on which measurements are taken—and yet taking the measurements has no physical effect on the photons. We can be sure of this, because the result holds true even if the decision about how to measure the electrons is taken after the experiment is over (but before any results are known).

Take a moment to digest this: The *actual physical result* is determined by our decision on how to make the measurements, even after the fact.

Again, this is not at all how objects behave, but it is the way information behaves. Our decision on which calculations to perform will determine what mathematical outcome we end up with, just as our decision on which measurements to make will determine whether the electron is expressed as a particle or a wave.

When we talk about a wave in this context, we're really talking about a probability wave—a distribution curve representing all possible positions that the electron might occupy at a given moment. And what is a probability wave except mathematical information? It is a graphical representation of all possible outcomes. What is a particle? It is one point on the graph—the one particular outcome that is actualized in any given case.

Things get even weirder. *In The Hidden Domain,* Norman Friedman observes:

> If we duplicate this experimental [double-slit] arrangement throughout the world with many experimenters, each firing just one electron at a given prearranged time, with each individual photographic plate showing the arrival of the one electron, and the results from all the plates are added together, then,

> amazingly, the interference pattern shows up again! These experiments are arranged so that no signal can travel between them at less than the speed of light, so there can be no physical communication between the electrons. Just how does each electron know where to strike the plate so that the interference pattern appears?

In a computational universe, the electrons know where to strike the plate because the calculations have already been performed at the level of information processing. The fact that the experiments are being carried out in different labs is irrelevant, because the source code is nonlocal. Since it is all one experiment (albeit broken up into different parts), the outcome is determined by a single set of calculations behind the scenes.

In other words, an electron behaves like a wave of probabilities when its position is not determined, and it behaves like a particle when its position is determined. What, then, is an electron? An object—or a mathematical construct, a bit of data?

There is more to the story. Every probability wave is essentially a menu of possible outcomes, each of which has an equal reality until the wave function "collapses" into a single outcome, which we call a particle. As long as the wave function is uncollapsed, its possibilities can branch out in a variety of possible futures. This branching or ramifying occurs in "virtual time," as distinct from the "real time" with which we're familiar. All of this is quite consistent with the computer model, in which all possible outcomes of the program exist in the source code but only one pathway can be followed by any given player.

Some physicists, troubled by the wave function's collapse, argue instead that all pathways are actualized in a constantly expanding collection of parallel universes or "many worlds." Like *Alice*'s White Queen, I can believe six impossible things before breakfast, but to think that whole universes sprout into being to match every possible path in a network of probabilities is more than I can swallow. What seems far more likely is that these alternate universes exist only in utero, as potentialities inherent in the source code; the informational pathways are real at the computational level, but most of them are not actualized at the experiential level. This would certainly be a lot more efficient than generating millions of new universes every second! As Elon Musk, quoted in Rizwan Virk's recent book *The Simulation Hypothesis,* puts it, "Quantum indeterminacy is really an optimization technique."

Another fascinating feature of the subatomic realm is quantum entanglement. Two electrons, once paired, will continue to affect each other no matter how far apart they travel, and can affect each other instantaneously—too fast for any signal to pass between them. If the spin of one electron is altered, the spin of its counterpart will be simultaneously altered in a corresponding way, even if the two electrons are at opposite ends of the universe.

If we think of electrons as objects, quantum entanglement is baffling. But if we think of them as pixels on a computer screen, the paradox disappears. A computer screen refreshes many times each second. The computer is constantly processing information, and with each screen refresh, the icons and graphics on the screen will be redrawn to reflect the latest calculations. The computer doesn't care if pixel A is on the extreme left side of the screen, and pixel B is on the extreme right side. The physical distance between the pixels is irrelevant to the information processor's calculations. If the "rule" is that a change in pixel A necessitates a complementary change in pixel B, then as soon as that calculation is made and the screen refreshes, both pixels will be appropriately altered.

Interestingly enough, the computer analogy also gives us a way to solve one of the world's oldest logical paradoxes—Zeno's paradox of the arrow. Zeno argued that motion is impossible. To prove it, he asked us to consider an arrow in flight. The arrow's path can be broken down into smaller and smaller units, and in the smallest of these units the arrow will be standing still. How, then, can it ever get anywhere, if its apparent motion consists ultimately of static positions? How can movement arise from immobility?

If Zeno had owned a PC, he might have solved his own paradox. The pixels on the screen never actually move. They are static. But because the screen is constantly refreshing, and because the pixels are drawn in different positions with each new refresh, the appearance of motion is created. The cursor appears to move across the screen, but it is really a series of still pictures being redrawn at a very high rate.

Let's say Zeno's arrow is equivalent to the cursor on the screen. As Zeno correctly stated, it is never actually in motion. But at a deeper level, our cosmic information processor is performing the necessary calculations and refreshing our space-time reality "screen," and it is those calculations and the resultant changes in the arrow's position that create movement as we know it.

This argument implies that all motion originates in the informational field, and that all apparent movement in our experiential reality is the result of "state transitions"—abrupt jumps from one state to another.

Quantum jumps and quantum tunneling are well-known examples of state transitions—discontinuous changes, in which a particle shifts its energy level or its position or from one state to another without passing through the intervening state. It would be like a person aging from ten years old to twelve years old without ever passing through age eleven, or like someone traveling directly east from New York City to Europe without crossing the Atlantic Ocean. It's not something that happens in our familiar reality, but it is easy enough to understand if the transitions reflect calculations taking place in an informational field. The particle does not need to pass through the intervening states, because it simply shifts from one state to another as a result of a behind-the-scenes calculation. The new state shows up as soon as the virtual-reality screen is refreshed.

For this to work, time itself must be "quantized"—there must be a minimum duration, corresponding to the length of time between screen refreshes. It is generally agreed that such a minimum duration exists. There is, first of all, a minimum physical distance known as the Planck length. Since the speed of light is unchanging, it is possible to calculate the time it takes light to travel one Planck length. This figure equals the Planck time constant, the shortest possible interval of time. In our model, the Planck length is equivalent to a single pixel on a computer screen, while the Planck time is equivalent to the time it takes to refresh the screen.

The speed of light, by the way, has also been singled out as an argument for the informational model. In his essay "The Physical World as a Virtual Reality," computer scientist Brian Whitworth asks, "Given the speed of light is a universal maximum, what is simpler, that it depends on the properties of featureless space, or that [it] represents a maximum network processing rate?" He suggests that the dilation of time predicted by Einstein's relativity theory can be seen as the information-processing system reaching the limits of its processing load.

The computational model can even be used to describe the origin of our space-time universe in the Big Bang. Whitworth observes that the Big Bang is not dissimilar to the "sudden influx of information" observed when a computer boots up. Maybe it should be called the Big Boot.

It has often been noted that the mathematical formulas necessary to describe our reality are confoundingly simple. Kepler's laws of motion and Einstein's $E=mc^2$ are remarkably elegant equations. There's no obvious reason why physical reality should be expressible in such terms. But if all physical things can be reduced to information, and if all physical events are the result of processing that information, then we might expect the basic rules governing the system to be as simple as possible. After all, these calculations would have to be performed untold quadrillions of times every second; simple formulas would clearly be better.

Now, I'm not saying our universe actually exists on the

hard drive of somebody's laptop. (If it does, I hope it's a Mac, because they don't crash as much.) This would be a purely materialistic interpretation of the idea—a way of locating the ground of being in some physical object, in this case an extradimensional or extraterrestrial (but physical) computer. I think the reality is far more subtle. Some of its nuances are caught in a famous quote from Stephen Hawking's *A Brief History of Time*: "Even if there is only one possible unified theory, it is just a set of rules and equations. What is it that breathes fire into the equations and makes a universe for them to describe?"

I suggest that what breathes fire into the equations is consciousness.

The data in a computer would just sit there, useless for game-playing purposes, unless the computer was able to render the data as images and sounds. By what means do we "render" our world? The most straightforward answer is: via our minds. Not our *brains*—brains are physical objects and thus part of the rendered, multidimensional, multisensory imagery we call reality. It is our *minds* that translate the informational code into the world of experience.

If so, then each individual mind renders its own "virtual-reality" world out of the same information matrix. And each "world" will be slightly different from all the others, because it will depend on our particular point of view—our focus, our choice of what to tune in and what to ignore.

If this idea sounds familiar, it may be because you're acquainted with the eighteenth-century philosopher Immanuel Kant. Kant divides reality into two realms—the phenomenal realm, or the world of appearances, and the noumenal realm, which consists of "things in themselves." For us, the phenomenal realm is the space-time cosmos, and the noumenal realm is the informational field.

Modern philosophers have been happy to accept Kant's phenomenal world, with its subjectivity and limitations, but are less interested in his noumenal world. The result is that Kantianism has given rise to modern epistemological skepticism, with no counterbalancing weight of the noumenal to ground it in a larger reality. In effect, philosophy has focused solely on the world of appearances. But I think Kant was closer to the mark. His bisection of the world into the noumenal and phenomenal realms is probably as close as we can get to understanding, in philosophical terms, what reality is all about.

In its entry on Kant, the *Stanford Encyclopedia of Philosophy* makes the important point that "Kant denies that appearances are unreal: they are just as real as things in themselves but are in a different metaphysical class." Similarly, in our model, it is not that the space-time cosmos is unreal; it is real for us. But it is not ultimately real; it is dependent on an informational field that is beyond space and time.

Kant wrote of "the objects, or what is the same thing, the experience in which alone they can be cognized (as given objects)." This profound statement encapsulates the often overlooked fact that *all experience is subjective*, and that what we call "physical things" are ultimately sensory images in our private field of awareness. Those sensory images—which include all perceptions, not just visual images—would not exist without an observer to perceive ("cognize") them. The informational field, on the other hand, exists regardless of any observer.

As the encyclopedia puts it,

> Whenever appearances do exist, in some sense they exist in the mind of human perceivers. So appearances are mental entities or mental representations ... These appearances cut us off entirely from the reality of things in themselves, which are non-spatial and non-temporal. Yet Kant's theory, on this interpretation, nevertheless requires that things in themselves exist, because they must transmit to us the sensory data from which we construct appearances.

This passage would require very little rewriting to apply to the VR model.

We all live in our own subjective bubble of experience, but we all draw on a common source. Each mind takes pure information and translates it into an experiential world, a world that is subjective but grounded in objective data. By *objective*, I mean that the informational field exists independent of the observer; by *subjective*, I mean that the rendered environment exists only in respect to the observer.

Now here's an interesting question. In this scenario, what is the role of physical space? Matter and energy are rendered from data. Data are nonphysical. The minds that do the rendering are also nonphysical. The resulting rendered sensory images appear to be physical, but they are only experiential constructs, the equivalents of avatars and icons on a computer screen. What exists in this model is not physical space but only information and consciousness. What we understand as physical space is only the shadow-show of mentally constructed images arising from an informational substrate.

It would appear that people like C.M.C. who have episodes of cosmic consciousness are able to temporarily break out of their mental bubble and tap into the informational field directly. In so doing, they feel they are exposed to all knowledge, which would be the case if the informational field constitutes all the data and programming that underlie what we call "the world." But they cannot retain most of the details when they return to ordinary consciousness, because they are back in their subjectively rendered mental space with its inherent limitations. Moreover, they are not *meant* to retain the details; they must remain fully immersed in the virtual-reality experience (Maya) so they can continue to participate in the cosmic play (Lila).

It is probable that many psychic events take place because the mind is able to tap into the informational field in a small way and access the source code directly. The source code, being nonphysical, is also nonlocal; information readily accessible in the matrix may pertain to physically separate and quite distant "objects," just as information in a computer may pertain to any object in any part of the screen. In this scenario, remote viewing and telepathy become quite possible and not "anomalous" at all.

Another implication of this notion of consciousness as the "render engine" of subjective reality is that each of us renders only that part of the world we perceive in any given moment. To conserve processing power, computer programs do not render images that are not currently on the screen. If you are playing a computer game and looking "north" at a mountain, the computer will render the mountain in all its detail, but it will not render the city behind you, to the "south." If you turn to face south, the computer will obediently render the city, but it will no longer render the mountain. In a virtual-reality environment, to be is to be perceived.

Does this mean that in the "real world," mountains and cities disappear if you're not looking at them? Logically, it does seem to follow that they *do* disappear from your particular reality bubble, your personal, subjective mental space. Your mind is not rendering those particular data into imagery at that moment. However, if the mountain or city is being observed by some other mind, then it is rendered in that mind's personal space. Moreover, the data that are the ultimate constituents of the mountain or city always exist in the source code, independent of any observer.

To ask an old question: Does the moon disappear if no one is looking at it? If literally no mind anywhere is observing the moon, then the moon is not currently being rendered in anybody's mental space, and in that sense it has "disappeared." But the data that give rise to the moon in the first place, the data of the informational field, are still there and are ready to be rendered by any mind at any time. So the moon is still there in the noumenal realm, but it is not presently being rendered in the phenomenal realm.

As the Zen master Yung-chia Ta-shih put it,

> The one Moon reflects itself wherever there is a sheet of water,

> And all the moons in the waters are embraced within the one Moon.

This idea ties in with, and may help explain, quantum indeterminacy. An electron's probability wave branches out into myriad pathways or "potentia," each representing a possible future. These pathways exist only at the computational level. Which future is actualized? Whichever one a mind selects. Once a mind has made the selection, the ramifying pathways collapse into a single defined value (an event known as "the collapse of the wave function"). This defined value will then be true for all observers—i.e., true in the rendered subjective environment of *any* mind. The defined value will be "reality."

Rizwan Virk envisions individual minds interacting in much the same way as the players of a massively multiplayer online role-playing game (MMORPG). Such games have

> the ability to store and track the state of a large number of simultaneous characters ... and the state of the shared, persistent game world as information. The information, which is the basis of everything that goes on in the virtual world, is stored somewhere outside the rendered world—on cloud servers that are invisible to those inside the world and rendered as needed ...
>
> Not only is a virtual world in modern MMORPGs larger than we can see on one screen, it isn't fully rendered into pixels until and unless it's necessary ... Only those places in the world where there is an

> observer get fully rendered as pixels ...
>
> MMORPGs are still rendered on individual computers—as such, a "shared rendered world" doesn't really exist. Each computer renders what is happening in your scene. If my character is present and yours is present, then both of our CPUs/GPUs will be rendering the scene based on shared information. Where is this information? It is both decentralized and centralized—it is sent from the client machines based upon every choice you make and then synchronized and sent to the other people that are in the same place that you are.

So here we are, nearing the end of our exploration of the first model. We can imagine our world as the product of a cosmic information processor—a nonphysical system existing outside of our space-time universe and governing the universe by means of the calculations it performs. Our everyday reality is analogous to the artificial reality of a computer game—except that, being fully immersed in it, we're unaware that it's a mere construct. Even our own bodies are part of this constructed reality and serve as our avatars, allowing our consciousness to explore and interact with this ever-changing environment.

There is no reason why the particular reality around us should be the only one that can be generated by the cosmic information processor. Indeed, most computer games have various levels of constructed reality; as you develop more skill, you advance to progressively higher levels, perhaps adopting a new avatar in order to better interface with new environments. And perhaps you reach a point where you no longer need to play the game, because you've seen through all its illusions. Perhaps you will take off the VR headset and delve into the source code directly, and in so doing, you will —to hijack another famous formulation of Stephen Hawking—"finally know the mind of God."

Maybe.

No doubt some objections have occurred to you as you've plowed through the above. I'll try to address the ones I've encountered when writing about this model on my blog.

The first objection. Haven't researchers proven that computers cannot create a simulation as complex as our cosmos?

Yes and no. Researchers have determined that quantum processes are too complex to simulate using classical computers. Since our universe is chock-full of quantum processes, this discovery rules out a giant classical computer crunching data behind the scenes. But when has anyone said that the simulation of our space-time cosmos has to be run on an old-school classical computer?

More important, our argument is not that the universe is literally created by a supercomputer, but rather that the world of appearances relates to an underlying noumenal reality in ways that can be analogized to a virtual reality world rendered from a program.

The second objection. Doesn't every generation try to model the world after current technology? When clockwork mechanisms were brand-new, the clockwork universe was in vogue. When holography was an exciting new field, we heard about the holographic universe. Now everything is computers and the Internet, so naturally we think of the universe in those terms.

There's a lot of truth to this. The clockwork universe did reflect the advanced technology of its day. But it also represented a considerable advance over earlier models. Perhaps as our leading-edge technology becomes more sophisticated, it more nearly approaches the underlying truths of cosmology. At the very least, it allows us to think about cosmology in more sophisticated terms.

The theory of the holographic universe popularized by physicist David Bohm is not all that different from the computational model. A holographic plate consists of wave-interference patterns. You can convert waves into data, or data into waves. It's possible to create a holographic plate by writing data on a computer, converting the data into wave functions, and engraving the waveforms on a plate. The process is known, logically enough, as computer-generated holography.

The point is that both the holographic model and the computational model see the space-time cosmos as an image projected or rendered out of an informational substrate. The exact nature of that informational source is still up for grabs.

The third objection. This whole idea is just too counterintuitive to be true.

Quantum physics itself is highly counterintuitive. Famed physicist Niels Bohr reportedly said, "Those who are not shocked when they first come across quantum theory cannot possibly have understood it." (Heisenberg, *Physics and Beyond*)

Even classical physics presents us with a startlingly different picture of our world. We may think of an object, such as a table, as a cluster of atoms bunched together, but in actuality the atoms are more like miniature solar systems widely separated in space. By far the greater part of the table is sheer emptiness. The table feels solid only because the atoms are bound together by electricity. When you touch a table, your body's electric field bumps up against the table's electric field, creating the impression of contact and solidity. There's a reason David Bohm called matter "condensed or frozen light." (Nichol, *Essential David Bohm*)

Any model of reality that takes classical physics, much less quantum physics, into account will necessarily be counterintuitive.

The fourth objection. Isn't it insensitive to compare the tragedies of life to a mere game? And how could any intelligently designed system allow for so much pain and suffering?

Life on earth is hard. There's no getting around this fact. Dr. Pangloss's encomia in *Candide* to "this best of all possible worlds" simply do not ring true for most of us. The "problem of pain" has vexed spiritual seekers of all descriptions. Why would a loving God or a beneficent universe allow so much suffering? The usual explanation, that original sin and plain old human cussedness are responsible, doesn't account for natural calamities such as earthquakes, tidal waves, and malarial mosquitoes. And human-caused evils like war and tyranny plague the innocent. So what's it all about?

One possible, though not altogether satisfactory, answer goes like this: How interesting or instructive would a role-playing game be without obstacles, hazards, and challenges? We seek conflict and drama in movies and novels—why not in the ultimate fictional story we've devised, the story of our own lives? As I can attest from personal experience, an author doesn't shrink from making things difficult for his characters; he knows that the more they struggle, the better the narrative. Our higher self, with a kind of pitiless creativity, lays traps and snares for us as we navigate the virtual environment of our personal drama. To us, it may seem like sadism, just as an animal may perceive nothing but hostile intent in the jab of the veterinarian's needle. It takes a higher intelligence to know that the pain of the injection is the necessary price of avoiding rabies—or that the pain of life on earth is necessary to teach us what we need to learn.

Here's another possible answer, which I prefer: While the game is planned in some respects, it may not be planned out in detail. If free will is real, then we, the players, can and will make pivotal decisions, writing our own script, which may deviate significantly from what the planners had in mind. Sometimes our higher self will nudge us back on track when we threaten to go too badly off course; other times, we're on our own. Like children learning to walk, we have to be allowed to fall.

But perhaps the best answer to the problem of pain is that the game, however real it seems while we are immersed in it, is *only* a game, and a brief one at that. It's a cliché that as people age, they look back on their lives and wonder where the time went. All those years look like only a moment; a lifetime seems like little more than a waking dream. I think this perception is correct. It *is* only a moment, only a dream.

The fifth objection. There's no such thing as a field of "pure information." Information exists only if there is a mind to perceive it.

This is how most of us think of information, but it's not how information theorists think of it. According to an online dictionary, information theory defines information as "a mathematical quantity expressing the probability of occurrence of a particular sequence of symbols, impulses, etc., as contrasted with that of alternative sequences." Mathematical quantities exist whether or not a mind conceives them. Or at least it can be argued that they do.

But doesn't information involve telling us something? And doesn't this necessarily involve a mind? Not exactly. Information theory got its start studying the transmission and reception of messages, but today it is understood that the message in question does not need to be sent or received by a mind. Messenger RNA, as its name implies, delivers messages, but that doesn't mean the ribosomes that receive the information have minds or understand what they're doing. Such messages can be compared to a key that fits a particular lock; the key does not know which lock it fits; the lock does not know that a key will open it; but when the right key finds the right lock, the "message" has been received.

In short, consciousness is not necessary for information to exist, when the term "information" is used in its technical sense.

The sixth objection. Maybe so, but the information still has to exist somewhere—encoded in DNA or in the pages of a book. Where is this alleged primordial field of pure information encoded?

It's true that an information matrix with no physical reality is inconceivable, in the sense that the human mind cannot visualize it. But then, we can hardly be expected to visualize anything outside the space-time universe in which we are fully immersed. If there is a deeper level to reality, that level is outside of space and time and is not definable in mundane terms.

Still, we could argue that there is another sort of "place," beyond genes and books, where information resides—namely, the mind. Imagine a cosmic Mind that eternally holds the entire source code in its field of awareness. This Mind (Brahman) would be the ground of being; the informational field is the content of this Mind; our personal consciousness is a small offshoot of the Mind; and our moment-to-moment experience of the physical universe is rendered out of the informational field by our consciousness as needed.

The seventh objection. I don't like this approach. It feels cold and impersonal.

Well, stay tuned! There are other models. In fact, "stay tuned" serves as a fitting segue into model number two.

CHAPTER TWO: THE SECOND MODEL

A continuum of frequencies

THE FIRST MODEL of postmortem existence I ever came across was the "transmission theory" offered by pioneering psychological theorist William James. James compares the brain to a receiver (in modern terms, think of a television set), which picks up a signal originating outside the device. If you change the channel, the receiver will pick up a different signal. If you damage the receiver, the reception will be distorted. If you turn off the receiver or smash it to pieces, it will no longer receive any signal, but the signal itself will continue unaffected. This simple model suggests how consciousness (analogized to a signal) can continue even when the brain (analogized to a receiver) is no longer operative.

A more sophisticated version of the transmission theory, presented by Bruce Lipton in *The Biology of Belief*, compares the brain to the Mars Rover and consciousness to signals transmitted from Mission Control. There is a back-and-forth relationship: the Rover uploads data to Mission Control, and Mission Control makes use of the data in deciding what instructions should be sent to the Rover. The Rover is also capable of a degree of autonomy; it can react to obstacles or hazards automatically, without waiting for instructions. Similarly, the brain provides a dataset to an extracerebral consciousness, which uses those data in formulating further instructions; and the more primitive parts of the brain are autonomous enough to react to stimuli without higher-level supervision.

Either way, it's a useful way of looking at things. But despite being called the transmission *theory*, it's not a true theory—not a testable scientific hypothesis. Neither is any one of the four models detailed in this book. All of them are metaphors, images, analogies. They aren't mechanistic explanations, only ways to make the phenomena easier to think about.

The transmission model uses the brain as the receiver. In this chapter I'd like to explore a different notion—that consciousness itself, rather than the brain, is what tunes in to and receives different frequencies.

Anyone who has encountered the Seth material channeled by Jane Roberts is already familiar with this idea. Seth repeatedly tells us that reality consists of many parallel channels, only one of which we occupy. There can be intrusions from other channels, resulting in anomalous phenomena.

My version of this model is simple enough. Think of your current reality as one frequency in a spectrum of frequencies, one channel on the dial. You are tuned to this channel and consider it normal. But if you move up or down the dial, you can tune to a different channel that is equally real, albeit unfamiliar. What is the *you* that does the tuning? Your faculty of consciousness. Moving into an altered state of consciousness can facilitate tuning to a new channel.

A tuner (say, in a radio) works by resonating at a particular frequency. It thus amplifies this frequency while ignoring the host of other frequencies occupying the same space. Turning the dial on an analog radio adjusts the tuner's resonance to a different frequency, allowing it to pick up a succession of higher or lower frequencies. The tuner and the signal it picks up must be "in sync," so to speak.

Without pressing the mechanical analogy too far, we can say that consciousness, corresponding to the tuner, must resonate at the appropriate reality-frequency. As consciousness is "dialed up," it will resonate at a higher frequency; if "dialed down," it will resonate at a lower frequency. The reality that is picked up will vary in frequency as consciousness itself varies in resonance. So consciousness and the reality it perceives must be "in sync."

As I said, simple. But in one respect this model is a bit tricky. We've already seen how Kant argued that the mind constructs the world of appearances, relying on categories of thought such as space and time, which don't exist in noumenal reality. If this is true, an altered state of consciousness should bring with it an altered world of appearances—a new reality, constructed in conformity to new mental categories. In other words, a change in our state of mind entails a change in our state of being.

To make this clearer, try to imagine a world unprocessed by consciousness. This is not actually possible; the closest we can get is the world described by physics. In that world, there is no color, only frequencies on the electromagnetic spectrum that can be translated into colors by eyes and brain. There is no sound, only frequencies that, when interpreted by ears and brain, can register as sounds. There is no solidity, only collections of atoms that produce an electrical field that repels other electrical fields, creating a boundary. There is no such thing as an atom, which is only a cloud of subatomic particles; and the particles themselves are not really particles but only probability distributions, a spread of potential outcomes.

And is there even this much, or are all these frequencies and fields and probabilities only ideas that exist in the mind?

Ultimately, consciousness and reality can be seen as only two sides of the same coin. A shift in consciousness equals a shift in reality. Different realities exist at different frequencies, and consciousness, too, operates at different frequencies. There is only a superficial difference between the perceiver and what is perceived.

Tuning in different channels on the spectrum, then, does not mean that we passively perceive whatever the next channel shows us. Rather, we *actively cooperate* in constructing the particular world of appearances that we are shown. We are always constructing our own personal reality, whether we are tuned to the ordinary, everyday channel familiar to us or tuned to a new channel that feels strange and different. Changing the channel changes *us*.

Let's look at some specific cases and see how the frequency model applies.

In April of 1880 a woman named Mrs. Crans had an out-of-body experience. Her daughter had died a few months earlier, leaving her son-in-law, Charley, a widower. She tells us:

> After lying down to rest, I remember feeling a drifting sensation, of seeming almost as if I was going out of the body. My eyes were closed; soon I realized that I was, or seemed to be, going fast some-

where. All seemed dark to me; suddenly I realized that I was in the room; then I saw Charley lying in a bed asleep; then I took a look at the furniture of the room, and distinctly saw every article—even to a chair at the head of the bed, which had one of the pieces broken in the back ... In a moment the door opened and my spirit-daughter Allie came into the room and stepped up to the bed and stooped down and kissed Charley. He seemed to at once realize her presence, and tried to hold her, but she passed right out of the room about like a feather blown by the wind ... The following Sunday I wrote, as was always my custom, to my son-in-law, Charley, telling him of all my experience, describing the room as I saw it finished.

It took a letter six days to go from here to Dakota, and the same length of time, of course, to come from there [to] here; and at the end of six days judge of my surprise to receive a letter from Charley telling me thus: "Oh, my darling mamma Crans! My God! I dreamed I saw Allie last Friday night!" He then described just as I saw her; how she came into the room and he cried and tried to hold her, but she vanished. Then at the end of six days, when my letter reached him, and he read of my similar experience, he at once wrote me that all I had seen was correct, even to every article of furniture in the room, also as his dream had appeared to him. (Myers, *Human Personality*)

Mrs. Crans lived in New York, while Charley Kernochan lived in Central City, Dakota. (The Dakota Territory was not split into the states of North and South Dakota until 1889.) Her out-of-body experience therefore involved a visitation to a place approximately 1500 miles away. Did she physically leave her own body and cross this distance?

I would say no. Instead, she found a way to tune in a different frequency. In her restful state, Mrs. Crans underwent a change in the resonance of her consciousness, which she perceived as "a drifting sensation ... almost as if I was going out of the body." As a result, she lost her emotional and intellectual connection with the body she perceived in her ordinary mental state, and became aware of a different body better suited to her new state of consciousness. This "new" body was not really new; it had been available to her all along, but she had not been aware of it, any more than a person listening to AM 770 can hear what's being broadcast on AM 820.

In this altered state, she experienced a sensation of speed ("I was, or seemed to be, going fast somewhere") because with her mind cleared of such limiting concepts as time and space, she could follow her thoughts without obstruction.

Her thoughts led her to her son-in-law's room, which she perceived with supernormal clarity, noting every detail of the furniture, even in the dark. With her consciousness tuning to a higher frequency, the nature and method of her perceptions shifted also.

Greatly enhanced perception is commonly reported in OBEs. In one case, an actor had an OBE while dancing on stage.

> Suddenly, without a moment's warning, I found myself in steel rafters near the ceiling of the room. I was aware of the gloom of the girders rising up through the shadows, and looking down on the spectacle below, I was startled to see that my vision had changed: I could see everything in the room—every hair on every head, it seemed—all at the same time. I took it all in, in a single omnipresent glance: hundreds of heads arranged in wavering rows of portable chairs, a half-dozen babies sleeping in laps, hairs of many different colors, shining from the light on stage. Then my attention shifted to the stage, and there we were in multicolored leotards, whirling about in our dance, and there I was—there I was—face-to-face with [my dancing partner]. (Ring, *Lessons from the Light*)

Compare this to the case of a woman who lost consciousness after she was rushed to the hospital with pneumonia:

> I was hovering over a stretcher in one of the emergency rooms at the hospital. I glanced down at the stretcher, knew the body wrapped in blankets was mine, and really didn't care. The room was much more interesting than my body. And what a neat perspective. I could see everything. And I do mean everything! I could see the top of the light on the ceiling, and the underside of the stretcher. I could see tiles on the ceiling and the tiles on the floor, simultaneously: three-hundred-degree spherical vision.

> And not just spherical. Detailed! I could see every single hair and the follicle out of which it grew on the head of the nurse standing beside the stretcher. At the time, I knew exactly how many hairs there were to look at. But I shifted focus. She was wearing glittery white nylons. Every single shimmer and sheen stood out in glowing detail, and once again, I knew exactly how many sparkles there were. (Ibid.)

Consider the supernormal perception reported by a drowning person who had an NDE:

> Suddenly I could see and hear as never before. The sound of a waterfall was so crisp and clear that it just cannot be explained by words. Earlier that year, my right ear had been injured ... But now I could hear perfectly clearly, better than I ever had before. My sight was even more beautiful. Sights that were close in distance were as clear as those far away, and this was at the same moment, which astounded me. There was no blurriness in my vision whatsoever. I felt as if I had been limited by my physical senses all these years, and that I had been looking at a distorted picture of reality. (Ibid.)

In *Light and Death*, cardiologist Michael Sabom introduced the now-famous case of Pam Reynolds, a musician who underwent an unusually powerful NDE during brain surgery. Reynolds said that during her NDE she was "the most aware that I think I have ever been in my life," and that her vision was "not like normal vision. It was brighter and more focused and clearer than normal vision," while her hearing "was a clearer hearing than with my ears."

Even more intriguing are cases of blind patients who reported visual perceptions in their NDEs. Vicki Umipeg, who was blind from birth, had two separate NDEs, one at the age of twenty after an attack of appendicitis, and the second at the age of twenty-two, following a car crash. She says, "Those two experiences were the only time I could ever relate to seeing, and to what light was, because I experienced it. I was able to see."

She described her second NDE to researcher Kenneth Ring. (The material in square brackets was added by Ring.)

> The first thing I was really aware of is that I was up on the ceiling, and I heard this doctor talking—it was a male doctor—and I looked down and I saw this body, and at first, I wasn't sure that it was my own. But I recognized my hair ... It was very long ... and it was down to my waist. And part of it had to be shaved off, and I remember being upset about that ... From up there on the ceiling, I could tell they were very concerned, and I could see them working on this body. I could see that my head was cut open. I could see a lot of blood [though she could not tell its color—she still has no concept of color, she says] ...
>
> I went up through the roof then. And that was astounding! ... It's like the roof ... just melted. (Ring, *Lessons from the Light*)

From that vantage point she saw "lights, and the streets down below, and everything." Her experience continued as she entered another dimension of reality. Ring summarizes:

> Now finding herself in an illuminated field, covered with flowers, she sees two children, long deceased, whom she had befriended when they were all in a school for the blind together. Then, they were both profoundly retarded, but in this state, they appear vital, healthy, and without their earthly handicaps. She feels a welcoming love from them and tries to move toward them. She also sees other persons whom she had known in life, but who have since died (such as her caretakers and her grandmother), and is drawn toward them, too.

Ring asked Vicki how her NDE compared to her dreams.

> VU: No similarity, no similarity at all.
>
> KR: Do you have any kind of visual perception in your dreams?
>
> VU: Nothing. No color, no sight of any sort, no shadows, no light, no nothing.
>
> KR: What kinds of perceptions are you aware of in your typical dreams?
>
> VU: Taste—I have a lot of eating dreams. And I have dreams when I'm playing the piano and singing, which I do for a living, anyway. I have dreams in which I touch things ... I taste things, touch things, hear things, and smell things—that's it.

KR: And no visual perceptions?

VU: No.

KR: So that what you experienced during your NDE was quite different from your dreams?

VU: Yeah, there's no visual impression at all in any dream I have.

This sense of heightened awareness isn't limited to physical perceptions; it can extend to supernormal knowledge, wisdom, and understanding, as in an NDE reported by famed psychologist Carl Jung:

> I had the certainty that I was about to enter an illuminated room and would meet there all those people to whom I belong in reality. There I would at last understand—this too was a certainty—what historical nexus I or my life fitted into. I would know what had been before me, why I had come into being, and where my life was flowing ... My life seemed to have been snipped out of a long chain of events, and many questions had remained unanswered. Why had it taken this course? Why had I brought these particular assumptions with me? What had I made of them? What will follow? I felt sure that I would receive an answer to all the questions. (Purrington, "Carl Jung's Near-Death Experience")

Irreducible Mind, an invaluable compendium of cases that challenge the status quo of modern materialism, quotes a cardiac arrest patient as saying, "I do not have words to express how vivid the [near-death] experience was. The main thing that stands out is the clarity of my thoughts during the episode." Also quoted is a six-year-old NDEr who called the experience "realer than real." "Realer than real" is how we might expect our experience to feel if we abruptly obtained access to a wider range of consciousness and perception.

Retired geologist Robert Crookall compiled numerous accounts of out-of-body experiences, which he called by the older term *astral projections*. Comparing the statements of OBErs with those communicated through mediums, Crookall writes:

> Both astral projectors and the 'dead' state that the physical body acts on the Soul Body, and therefore on the Soul and on consciousness, after the manner of the "blinkers" on the harness of a horse, or like a damper, a blanket, a sphincter, etc.: it narrows, focuses and retards our thought and emotions. This statement accords with another (made independently) that when the physical body is shed, either temporarily, as in astral projection, or permanently, at death, thought and feeling is much more rapid and more intense ... [Case] No. 20 similarly said, "You may think that you can think and act with rapidity—but once you have become conscious in the astral body you will realize at what a snail's pace the conscious mind moves in comparison." ...
>
> The "communicator" of E.C. Randall ... said that all the mental actions of mortals are "intensified to a degree you cannot imagine" once the blinkers-like

> body is cast off. [In another channeled communication,] "Julia" told W.T. Stead, "Material senses are not so much to help us to see and hear as to bar us off from seeing and hearing. We are on earth, as it were, with blinkers on ... Death is more of a laying-down of the blinkers that limited and confined our vision than almost anything else." (Crookall, *More Astral Projections*)

All of this is broadly consistent with the idea that our range of consciousness is ordinarily restricted, but with a shift in mental focus corresponding to a change of resonance, we can tune in other frequencies, receiving them with unusual clarity.

Getting back to Mrs. Crans, not only did she perceive the room and her son-in-law, she was also able to perceive the spirit form of her daughter. How could she see entities from two different realities—physical and spiritual—at the same time? I suggest that, in a transitional state between the two realities, she was able to tune in both channels at once, much as a radio or TV may pick up two stations whose signals overlap. In TV, this phenomenon is known as "ghosting," which is quite apropos for our purposes. Ghosts sightings of all sorts—apparitions, hauntings, poltergeists—may result from tuning in more than one frequency simultaneously, so that our mind constructs a world of appearances incorporating elements from multiple frequencies.

Apparitions are much more commonly reported than we may realize. Many of the most dramatic cases involve crisis apparitions, an extensively documented phenomenon in parapsychology, in which someone sees the apparition of a loved one and later learns that the loved one in question was in peril, dying, or newly deceased at that time.

It's an evening in the nineteenth century, and you're relaxing at home, reading a book in a dreamy reverie. Looking up from the book, you receive a shock.

> I distinctly saw a school-friend of mine, to whom I was very much attached, standing near the door. I was about to exclaim at the strangeness of her visit when, to my horror, there were no signs of anyone in the room but my mother. I related what I had seen to her, knowing she could not have seen, as she was sitting with her back towards the door, nor did she hear anything unusual, and was greatly amused at my scare, suggesting I had read too much or been dreaming.
>
> A day or so after this strange event, I had news to say my friend was no more. The strange part was that I did not even know she was ill, much less in danger so could not have felt anxious at the time on her account, but may have been thinking of her; that I cannot testify. Her illness was short, and death very unexpected. Her mother told me she spoke of me not long before she died ... She died the same evening and about the same time that I saw her vision, which was the end of October, 1874. (Rogo, "Psychical Research")

I once saw a skeptic argue against crisis apparitions on the ground that the percipient was in a crisis and therefore his perceptions could not be trusted. This betrays a misunderstanding of the concept. It is not the perceiver who is in crisis, but the person whose ghostly form is seen. The perceiver is typically in a relaxed state, perhaps daydreaming or on the verge of sleep. This state of mind seems especially prone to inducing psychic impressions, as has been shown by the Ganzfeld tests, an extensive series of international experiments in which volunteers are placed in a state of mild sensory deprivation in order to boost their latent telepathic abilities.

Apparitions vary in their degree of corporeality; some seem wispy and insubstantial, while others are reported to be solid and tangible. In cases where an apparition has been observed by several people at once, it is typically seen from various perspectives, like any other physical thing; the person facing the apparition will see it head on, while the person standing to the side will see it in profile. Apparitions also have been seen reflected in mirrors, and they can match the light-and-shadow conditions of their environment. In some cases, apparitions seem to have been caught on film, videotape, or other recording media, while the field of electronic voice phenomena offers many examples (admittedly often disputed and in many instances spurious) of voices captured from the ether.

In short, apparitions can seemingly have the physical characteristics we associate with ordinary objects. And yet they are not ordinary physical objects, because they walk through walls, appear and vanish unpredictably, and sometimes are seen by only certain observers while remaining invisible to others. They behave like intrusions from another channel of reality that are picked up by our consciousness (if it is in the proper state of receptivity) and interpreted as part of our reality.

If we can see apparitions of the departed when our consciousness is tuned to the right frequency, can the departed see us? It appears they can, at least in cases of earthbound spirits—deceased persons who have not made a full transition to the spiritual plane. The idea is familiar to many people today because of the movie *The Sixth Sense*, but it has been around for a long time and is surprisingly well supported. Dr. Carl Wickland, director of a psychiatric hospital, became convinced that many of his psychotic patients were victims of obsessing spirits who, in most cases, did not know they were dead. Confused and disoriented, they had latched on to living persons without quite knowing what they were doing. Through the mediumship of his wife, Wickland talked to these spirits and informed them of their circumstances. When the spirits were persuaded, they literally "saw the light." Over and over again, they reported seeing a bright light previously invisible to them, and they found themselves in the company of loved ones who escorted them to a higher plane. In his memoir *Thirty Years Among the Dead*, Wickland maintained that patients treated in this way recovered their senses, even when other treatments had failed.

In terms of the frequency model, earthbound spirits are stuck between channels, able to perceive living persons and also some other spirits. Their confused state of mind is reflected, or manifested, in a confused, dreamlike reality.

If death is merely switching from one channel to another,

we would expect people who have initiated the dying process to report just such changes in their consciousness and their accompanying reality. They do. The literature of near-death experiences includes many OBEs similar to that of Mrs. Crans, as well as explorations of even more unfamiliar states of being. Here's one from more than a century ago.

The case was reported by a medical doctor, A.S. Wiltse of Skiddy, Kansas, who in 1889 contracted typhoid fever and entered a coma. Though close to death, he ultimately recovered. When he awakened, he startled those who were attending him by insisting on relating an unusual experience "despite all injunctions to be quiet."

Eight weeks after "the day I died," Wiltse wrote a lengthy paper about it, which was published in a medical journal. In it, Wiltse wrote, "There are plenty of witnesses to the truth of the above statements, in so far as my physical condition was concerned. Also to the fact that just as I described the conditions about my body and in the room, so they actually were. I must, therefore, have seen things by some means." Later, he obtained sworn depositions from some witnesses.

What happened to Dr. Wiltse? Let him tell us:

> I passed about four hours in all without pulse or perceptible heartbeat, as I am informed by Dr. S.H. Raynes, who was the only physician present. During a portion of this time several of the bystanders thought I was dead, and such a report being carried outside, the village church bell was tolled. Dr. Raynes informs me, however, that by bringing his eyes close to my face, he could perceive an occasional

short gasp, so very light as to be barely perceptible, and that he was upon the point, several times of saying, "He is dead," when a gasp would occur in time to check him ...

I lost, I believe, all power of thought or knowledge of existence in absolute unconsciousness. I came again into a state of conscious existence and discovered that I was still in the body, but the body and I had no longer any interest in common. I looked in astonishment and joy for the first time upon myself—the me, the real Ego, while the not-me closed it up on all sides like a sepulcher of clay.

With all the interest of a physician, I beheld the wonders of my bodily anatomy, intimately interwoven with which, even tissue for tissue, was I, the living soul of that dead body ... I watched the interesting process of the separation of soul and body. By some power, apparently not my own, the Ego was rocked to and fro, laterally, as a cradle is rocked, by which process its connection with the tissues of the body was broken up. After a little time the lateral motion ceased, and along the soles of the feet beginning at the toes, passing rapidly to the heels, I felt and heard, as it seemed, the snapping of innumerable small cords. When this was accomplished, I began slowly to retreat from the feet, toward the head, as a rubber cord shortens ...

As I emerged from the head, I floated up and down and laterally like a soap bubble attached to the bowl of a pipe until I at last broke loose from the body and fell lightly to the floor, where I slowly arose and expanded into the full stature of a man. I seemed to be translucent, of a bluish cast and perfectly naked. With a painful sense of embarrassment, I fled toward the partially opened door to escape the eyes of the two ladies whom I was facing, as well as others who I knew were about me, but upon reaching the door I found myself clothed, and satisfied upon that point, I turned and faced the company. As I turned, my left elbow came in contact with the arm of one of two gentlemen, who were standing at the door. To my surprise, his arm passed through mine without apparent resistance, the severed parts closing again without pain, as air re-unites. I looked quickly up at his face to see if he had noticed the contact, but he gave no sign, only stood and gazed toward the couch I just left. I directed my gaze in the direction of his, and saw my own dead body. It was lying just as I had taken so much pains to place it, partially upon the right side, the feet close together and the hands clasped across the breast. I was surprised at the paleness of the face. I had not looked in a glass for some days and had imagined that I was not as pale as most very sick people are ...

I now attempted to gain the attention of the people [in the room] with the object of comforting them as well as assuring them of their own immortality. I bowed to them playfully and saluted with my right hand. I passed about among them also, but found that they gave me no heed. Then the situation struck me as humorous and I laughed outright.

They certainly must have heard that, I thought, but it seemed otherwise, for not one lifted their eyes from my body. It did not once occur to me to speak and I concluded the matter by saying to myself: "They see only with the eyes of the body. They cannot see spirits. They are watching what they think is I, but they are mistaken. That is not I. This is I and I am as much alive as ever."

I turned and passed out at the open door, inclining my head and watching where I set my feet as I stepped down on to the porch.

I crossed the porch, descended the steps, walked down the path and into the street. Then I stopped and looked about me. I never saw that street more distinctly than I saw it then. I took note of the redness of the soil and of the washes the rain had made. I took a rather pathetic look about me, like one who is about to leave his home for a long time. Then I discovered that I had become larger than I was in earth life and congratulated myself thereupon. I was somewhat smaller in the body than I just liked to be, but in the next life, I thought, I am to be as I desired ...

"How well I feel," I thought. "Only a few minutes ago I was horribly sick and distressed. Then came that change, called death, which I have so much dreaded. It is past now, and here I am still a man, alive and thinking, yes, thinking as clearly as ever, and how well I feel; I shall never be sick again. I have no more to die." ... I discovered then a small cord, like a spider's web, running from my shoulders back to my body and attaching to it at the base of the neck in front ...

[After losing consciousness for a second time] I again awoke [and] found myself in the air, where I was upheld by a pair of hands, which I could feel pressing lightly against my sides. The owner of the hands, if they had one, was behind me, and shoving me through the air at a swift but a pleasant rate of speed. By the time I fairly realized the situation I was pitched away and floated easily down a few feet, alighting gently upon the beginning of a narrow, but well-built roadway, inclined upward at an angle of something less than 45 degrees ...

[After a walk up the road] I saw at some distance ahead of me three prodigious rocks blocking the road, at which sight I stopped, wondering why so fair a road should be thus blockaded, and while I considered what I was to do, a great and dark cloud, which I compared to a cubic acre in size, stood over my head. Quickly it became filled with living, moving bolts of fire, which darted hither and thither through the cloud. They were not extinguished by contact with the cloud. I could see them as one sees fish in deep water.

I was aware of a presence, which I could not see, but which I knew was entering into the cloud from the southern side. The presence did not seem, to my mind, as a form, because it filled the cloud like some vast intelligence ... Then from the right side and from the left of the cloud a tongue of black vapor shot forth and rested lightly upon either side of my head, and as they touched me thoughts not my own entered into my brain ...

The following is as near as I can render [these thoughts]:

"This is the road to the internal world. Yonder rocks are the boundary between the two worlds and the two lives. Once you pass them, you can no more return into the body. If your work is complete on earth, you may pass beyond the rocks. If, however, upon consideration you conclude that ... it is not done, you can return into the body." ...

[After reasoning it out, I decided] "now that I am so near I will cross the line and stay." So determining I moved cautiously along the rocks [and] advanced [my] left foot across the line. As I did so, a small, densely black cloud appeared in front of me and advanced toward my face. I knew that I was to be stopped. I felt the power to move or to think leaving me. My hands felt powerless at my side, my head dropped forward, the cloud touched my face and I knew no more.

Without previous thought and without apparent effort on my part, my eyes opened. I looked at my hands and then at the little white cot upon which I was lying, and realizing that I was in the body, in astonishment and disappointment, I exclaimed: "What in the world has happened to me? Must I die again?" (Myers, *Human Personality*)

This 1889 case has much in common with recent NDEs, showing that the phenomenon is by no means a new development, although advances in medical technology have made it more common. Although some people may reject it because of its age, I actually find this a point in its favor. Dr. Wiltse was writing long before the near-death experience was popularized as a cultural trope. He couldn't have been influenced by the spate of books, movies, and TV shows that followed Raymond Moody's groundbreaking 1975 book *Life After Life*, which introduced NDEs to the general public and even coined the term *near-death experience.*

Dr. Wiltse's account has the virtue of being uncontaminated by any modern cultural influences. And it is quite compatible with the frequency model.

As his body failed, Dr. Wiltse experienced a blackout, during which his consciousness shifted to a different frequency. In his altered state, he no longer identified with the physical body ("I was still in the body, but the body and I had no longer any interest in common"). As he became accustomed to this new condition, his altered perceptions generated a new reality for him—a spirit body, one that suited his mental image of himself by being healthier (and taller!) than the body he'd left. That his new body was a mental construction is shown by the fact that, in response to his embarrassment at being naked, he suddenly found himself fully clothed.

Like Mrs. Crans, or like the earthbound spirits interrogated by Dr. Wickland, he could still see the living people around him, even though they could not see him. Also like Mrs. Crans and others, his perception of physical reality was greatly enhanced ("I never saw that street more distinctly"). Unlike Mrs. Crans, the doctor saw a threadlike cord running from his spirit body to his physical body. This feature, frequently observed in both NDEs and OBEs, seems to be the mind's way of representing the as-yet-unbroken connection between two levels of consciousness and reality.

Dr. Wiltse was not through with his shifts in consciousness. He suffered a second blackout and awoke to an impression of traveling at speed, as we saw with Mrs. Crans. It is noteworthy that he conceived of being held by hands but didn't see any. I would argue that his impression of being carried in that way was his mind's interpretation, a holdover from his habitual state of consciousness, in which gravity cannot be defied without some explanation.

This second shift of consciousness brought him to a still higher frequency level, visualized as being high in the sky, and allowed him to perceive a spiritual realm with many features in common with those reported in other NDEs—a path, a barricade, a being of light who communicates telepathically and presents the experiencer with a choice.

As is often the case in other NDEs, the choice does not seem to have been altogether genuine, because even after Dr. Wiltse chose to remain in the afterlife, he was still impelled back into the body.

I would argue that Dr. Wiltse's entire experience of a spiritual realm, barricade, and "vast intelligence" was every bit as real as your experience of reading this book right now. It was simply a different level of reality accessed by a different level of consciousness. It was a different set of perceptions, allowing for a different experience of reality, made possible by a different fine-tuning of his mental state. The elements were both familiar and unfamiliar. There were a road and boulders and a cloud, all of which we might experience on earth, but there were also strange flashes of light and telepathic communication from a superhuman intelligence. He was at some halfway point between familiar reality and a higher, unfamiliar reality. The barricade or boundary represented the threshold to a further adjustment of consciousness that would allow for a different and no doubt less familiar experience.

Dr. Wiltse suffered yet another blackout at the conclusion of his adventure. When he came to, he was back in the body—in other words, his consciousness had reverted to its familiar frequency, and his reality had similarly reverted to his accustomed set of perceptions and mental categories. His reaction was not unusual in such cases; he was disappointed, even distressed, at having enjoyed a glimpse of an expanded consciousness (and a wider reality), only to be "dialed back" to the limitations and imperfections of ordinary subjective existence.

But how do we know that the experiences of Mrs. Crans, Dr. Wiltse, and so many others are not hallucinations? To go further, if Kant is right in saying that consciousness processes our perceptions according to preexisting mental categories, how can we be sure that *any* of our experiences are not hallucinations? How can we trust our perceptions at all?

A thoroughgoing skeptic would say we can't, but no one actually lives by this dictum. In practice, we accept our perceptions as accurate—or at least accurate enough—most of the time. Yet we're aware that we can be fooled by optical illusions or by mental changes brought on by drugs, illness, or injury. Our practical method of determining what's true is mainly based on consensus. If you're the only one who sees an elephant galloping down the freeway, you may be imagining it. If other people see it too, you're on safer ground. This is the value of what's known in parapsychology as *veridical experiences*—experiences that are independently confirmed by the reports of others.

In the case of Mrs. Crans, we have two veridical components. One is her accurate description of Charley's room, 1500 miles from where she rested, as confirmed by Charley himself. The other is her description of her late daughter's appearance and actions, again seconded by Charley. Adding credibility to the account is that Charley reported the spiritual visitation even before receiving his mother-in-law's letter.

In the case of Dr. Wiltse, we have the statements of the attending physician, Dr. Raynes, and other witnesses, which Wiltse took the trouble to collect, verifying his description of the people present in the room and their behavior. He even obtained sworn depositions from some of them. An additional factor is Wiltse's medical condition; Dr. Raynes reported that Wiltse was so deeply comatose, he showed no response to a needle thrust deeply into his flesh. Even ordinary mental processes should not be possible in such a condition, let alone the detailed, verifiable observations Wiltse reported.

Finally, there's the issue of commonality between his account and many others. If one explorer returns from an unknown continent and makes a report, we may be skeptical; if dozens, hundreds, or thousands of other explorers unconnected with each other deliver similar reports, we are entitled to accept the basic truth of what they're saying, even if there are discrepancies and variations among their experiences.

If Wiltse were the only person ever to report leaving his body when critically ill, closely observing the deathbed scene, or finding himself in a spirit world, we might chalk up his account to an overactive imagination. But his is only one of countless reports, some of which are even better attested. Despite differences in the experiences that have been related, enough common elements have emerged to form a recognizable pattern. These elements include:

- Disconnecting both emotionally and literally from the body, often with the parallel development of a "soul body" that can hover in air and pass through solid objects, and which may be connected to the physical body by a cord.
- Observations of one's environment, typically with greatly enhanced perception.
- A frustrating inability to communicate with the living.
- A feeling of health, relief, and "exuberance" (Wiltse's word).
- Transition to a different plane of reality, accomplished by rapid flight.
- An earthlike quality to this other reality (a road, flowers, trees).
- A barrier blocking further progress.
- A cloud or a bright light embodying a higher intelligence, which communicates telepathically with the experiencer.

- A choice to remain or return, based on whether or not one's work on earth is complete.
- The sudden resumption of life in the physical body, often accompanied by surprise and disappointment.
- A compelling need to relate the experience.

All these elements are present in Wiltse's account. Other common elements in NDEs, not seen in the Wiltse case, include:

- A transition through a tunnel or other passageway.
- A reunion with departed loved ones, who communicate telepathically.
- An encounter with one or more religious figures, usually consistent with the experiencer's personal belief system or background.
- Temporary merging with a higher intelligence in which the meaning of life is made clear.
- A comprehensive review of one's life, in which the experiencer directly feels the impact of his actions on other people, for better or worse.
- Lasting changes in one's personality, behavior, and philosophy.

Some patterns are cultural. NDEs in the Western world often involve a choice, as in the Wiltse case. NDEs in India typically exclude the idea of choice or a personal mission that must be completed on earth, and instead present the person's brush with the afterlife as a clerical mistake, a bureaucratic mishap. Often a different person of the same name was scheduled to die that day, and some angelic bumbler picked up the wrong one!

Do I think clerical mistakes of that sort really happen? No. Nor am I convinced that the experiencer has a genuine choice about whether or not to resume earthly life. (As noted, Dr. Wiltse's choice proved illusory; his choice to remain was overruled.) And I'm dubious of encounters with iconic religious figures like Jesus or the Virgin Mary, which constitute a minority of NDE reports.

In all these cases, we need to remember that our personal reality is constructed out of mental categories consistent with the "vibrational level" of our consciousness. (When psychics, mediums, and mystics talk about "raising their vibrations," their statements can be readily understood in terms of adjusting their resonance in order to tune in a higher frequency.) If we encounter an unfamiliar situation that we are not fully prepared for, we construct a reality—a narrative—that makes sense of it in terms we understand. A person undergoing an NDE is temporarily caught between frequencies, having made only a partial transition from one level of consciousness to the next; as such, he lacks the ability to fully process and interpret what's happening to him. Any familiar-seeming and superficially logical interpretation may be sufficient to get him safely through the experience and back on firmer ground. Think of the invisible hands that Dr. Wiltse imagined carrying him through space. The "hands" helped make the experience intelligible to him.

Despite cultural and idiosyncratic personal differences, NDEs do exhibit striking similarities from case to case, even over the centuries. Medieval NDEs were reported. In his painting *Ascent to the Empyrean*, Hieronymus Bosch depicted souls ascending into a tunnel that led to a bright light. If an NDE were only a kind of dream, why would everyone's dreaming be so similar? But if NDEs are a function of tuning in a higher channel on the spectrum, we would expect broad areas of agreement.

NDEs, OBEs, and apparitions are by no means the only possible instances of tuning to another frequency. As we've seen, mediums speak of raising their vibrations—and their communicators are equally consistent in saying they must lower their vibrations to get through.

In other words, the communicator, in order to get in touch with physical reality, must dial down the range of his consciousness, limiting it to a particular part of the spectrum. In the process, consciousness itself is artificially restricted or constrained. A great deal of the mental strain reported by communicators is probably attributable to the difficulty of maintaining this restricted range of consciousness. Garbled or incomplete messages, in some cases, are probably the result of being temporarily confined to a narrow range of consciousness or being unable to maintain that focus.

The banality or incoherence of many mediumistic communications has long been a sore point among skeptics, who say that if people could communicate from beyond, they would have better things to talk about than personal trivia. I think this criticism is often mistaken, inasmuch as personal trivia are necessary to establish a communicator's identity. How would a disembodied person prove he is who he says he is, except by recalling trivial details known only to himself and his loved ones?

But what about the confusion so often evident in these sittings? Why are so many messages nonsensical or diffuse? This hardly seems like evidence of an expanded consciousness. Some people have been known to grumble that if postmortem existence is this mindless, it would be better not to survive at all.

It's not a recent opinion. The ancient Greeks believed the dead were consigned to Hades, where they existed as shadowy wraiths with only a trace of their former personality. The ancient Hebrews, with their occasional references to the shadowland of Sheol, seem to have held a similar view. I suspect that both viewpoints originated in the séances of that time, when communicators came through haltingly or incoherently.

We need to distinguish between the communicator's actual mental capacities and the message that is received. By all accounts, mediumship is a tricky business for those at both ends of the process—the medium herself and the discarnate communicator. Many communicators have complained that their efforts are like trying to be heard through a barrier. The most famous example is a purported communication from F.W.H. Myers after his death, bemoaning the difficulties of automatic (spirit-controlled) writing:

> Yet another attempt to run the blockade—to strive to get a message through—how can I make your hand docile enough—how can I convince them?
>
> The nearest simile I can find to express the difficulties of sending a message is that I appear to be standing behind a sheet of frosted glass—which blurs sight and deadens sound—dictating feebly—to

> a reluctant and somewhat obtuse secretary.
>
> A terrible feeling of impotence burdens me. (Blum, *Ghost Hunters*)

George Pellew, whom we met in the Introduction, conveyed this message through Mrs. Piper:

> Remember we share and always shall have our friends in the dreamlife, *i.e.* your life so to speak, which will attract us for ever and ever, and so long as we have any friends *sleeping* in the material world; you to us are more like as we understand sleep, you look shut up as one in prison, and in order for us to get into communication with you, we have to enter into your sphere, as one like yourself, sleep. This is just why we make mistakes, as you call them, or get confused and muddled. (Myers, *Human Personality*)

Richard Hodgson, Mrs. Piper's chief investigator, mused that the communicator, especially in his early attempts, might be hampered by the strangeness of his circumstances:

> The state might be like that of awakening from a prolonged period of unconsciousness into strange surroundings. If my own ordinary body could be preserved in my present state, and I could absent myself from it for days or months or years, and continue my existence under another set of conditions altogether, and if I could then return to my own

> body, it might well be that I should be very confused and incoherent at first in my manifestations by means of it. How much more would this be the case where I to return to *another* human body. I might be troubled with various forms of aphasia and agraphia, might be particularly liable to failures of inhibition, might find the conditions oppressive and exhausting, and my state of mind would probably be of an automatic and dreamlike character. Now the communicators through Mrs. Piper's trance exhibit precisely the kind of confusion and incoherence which it seems to me we have reason to expect if they are actually what they claim to be. (Ibid.)

It's important to note that many communications are not banal. Practiced communicators have offered elaborate disquisitions on life, reality, and the meaning of things. Skeptics find the content of these messages too abstract and unverifiable to have any evidential value. So if the messages are deeply personal, they're dismissed for being trivial; if they're wide-ranging and philosophical, they're dismissed for being vague. Heads they win, tails we lose.

If consciousness can tune in other frequencies, we might expect other kinds of phenomena besides those we've already considered. For instance, savant syndrome.

Savants are people with neurological disabilities who are capable of amazing, sometimes inexplicable mental feats. Often these are feats of memory. Kim Peek memorized 12,000 books, reading one page with his left eye and the facing page with his right eye. A nineteenth-century patient memorized all of Gibbon's monumental *Rise and Fall of the Roman Empire* and could recite it both backward or forward, but he did not understand a word of it. One autistic savant memorized the value of pi to 22,514 decimal places.

Other abilities involve more than memorization. Autistic twins George and Charles can tell you what day of the week falls on any given date over 40,000 years (past or future). They can also tell you when Easter was celebrated in any year, information that ought to require complex mathematical computations. Some savants can retain vast quantities of information after only brief exposure. Following a fifteen-minute helicopter ride over London, Stephen Wiltshire drew a twelve-foot-long panorama of seven square miles of the city with photographic accuracy.

Most impressive are creative abilities that go well beyond computation and recall. Darold A. Treffert, author of *Islands of Genius,* tells us:

> Leslie Lemke is blind, severely cognitively impaired and has cerebral palsy. Yet he played back Tchaikovsky's Piano Concerto No. 1 flawlessly after hearing it for the first time at age 14. Leslie ... has never had a music lesson in his life.
>
> Matt Savage ... very quickly mastered the piano at age 6 1/2 and had his first CD of jazz competition at age 8. Matt is recognized worldwide now as "the Mozart of Jazz" ... He recently recorded his eighth CD.
>
> Alonzo Clemens was not born a savant. Instead his spectacular sculpting abilities emerged after a child-

> hood fall and brain injury. Alonzo, from that time forward, could look at a picture of an animal in a magazine, or see an animal at the zoo, and then sculpt that animal, in about an hour or so, using the oil-based clay which he molds so quickly and artistically with his gifted hands.

Typically, these abilities seem to come out of nowhere, defying explanation. It is almost as if the savant is channeling the skill from an external source. Take the case of Jay:

> By age five Jay had composed five symphonies. His Fifth Symphony, which was 190 pages and 1328 bars in length, was professionally recorded by the London Symphony Orchestra for Sony Records. On [a] *60 Minutes* program in 2006 Jay's parents stated that Jay spontaneously began to draw little cellos on paper at age two. Neither parent was particularly musically inclined, and there were never any musical instruments, including a cello, in the home. At age three Jay asked if he could have a cello of his own. The parents took him to a music store and to their astonishment Jay picked up a miniature cello and began to play it. He had never seen a real cello before that day. After that he began to draw miniature cellos and placed them on music lines. That was the beginning of his composing ...
>
> Jay says that the music just streams into his head at lightning speed, sometimes several symphonies running simultaneously. "My unconscious directs

my conscious mind at a mile a minute," he told the correspondent on that program.

In another case,

> A forty-year-old motivational speaker dives into a shallow pool and sustains a major concussion. When he recovers, he is able to play the piano and guitar, neither of which he could play pre-injury. He now composes movie soundtracks and makes his living performing professionally.

Treffert notes,

> Prodigious savants particularly seem to "know things they never learned." Leslie [Lemke], for example, who has never had a music lesson in his life, and cannot read music because he is blind, innately and instinctively seems to know the "rules of music" according to professional musicians who have met and listen to him. An experienced music professor said about Matt [Savage], "he seems to know things that are beyond his own existence." Other prodigious savants, without exposure or training, also innately "know" the rules of music, art, mathematics or calendar calculating.

Oliver Sacks, in his account of the autistic twins, imagined them seeing the dates of the calendar as an "immense mnemonic tapestry, a vast (or possibly infinite) landscaping in which everything could be seen, either isolated or in relation," while Treffert says savants "seem to 'see' their answers as if projected on to a screen."

Even paranormal abilities such as ESP are reported in the literature, though most writers shy away from giving them any credence. Exceptions are psychiatrist Diane Powell (2006), who invokes quantum entanglement as a possible explanation of psi in savants, and Keith Chandler (2004), who acknowledges the paranormal nature of some savants' ability "to remember things they never learned." (Both sources are referenced in Treffert, *Islands of Genius*.)

Treffert himself opts for a biological answer, genetic memory—essentially an inheritance of information that, he thinks, can explain cases of xenoglossy (the sudden ability to speak a foreign language one has not been exposed to), overnight proficiency in musical play and composition, and an implicit understanding of the rules of higher mathematics:

> What I define as genetic memory does not include reincarnation, mysticism, existential ruminations, transcendentalism or paranormal phenomena. Indeed it is a concept even much narrower than Jung's "collective unconscious." Genetic memory is simply the biological transfer of *knowledge, templates, and certain skills* along with the myriad of other inherited physical characteristics, instincts, traits and behaviors. (emphasis in original)

But it's hard to see how even one's own memories of how to play the piano, calculate remote dates, or speak a foreign language could be encoded in DNA. It's even harder to imagine these encoded memories being genetically transferred down through the generations and epigenetically activated on demand. A more likely solution, albeit one that flies in the face of materialist assumptions, is that the savant adjusts the resonance of his or her consciousness to tune to a different frequency of reality, one in which the necessary information already exists and can be tapped directly. This could help explain the narrow range of most savants' abilities—they are able to access only specific frequencies—and the self-described feeling of having music, facts, and figures "stream into [one's] head." When Oliver Sacks visualizes the savant as gazing on a tapestry, or an infinite landscape, which contains all the answers, he may not be far off; the tapestry or landscape is the higher frequency dialed in by consciousness.

Even the mind-boggling talents of savants don't exhaust the possibilities of the frequency model. Briefly, let's consider some other mystifying phenomena.

Telepathy. Tuning in to another mind may be no different from tuning in to another reality. In each case, if consciousness resonates at the right frequency, it will sync up with the signal.

Alien abductions are very much like OBEs, except that the "abductee" interprets the experience in physical terms. Instead of leaving the body and floating through a wall, he imagines his physical body rising up and floating off. How can he make sense of this situation? For moderns steeped in science-fiction, the idea of extraterrestrial super-technology comes to mind. Obligingly, the experience as constructed by his mind follows the patterns of a sci-fi story: vaguely malevolent aliens in a flying saucer conduct incomprehensible and scary experiments.

UFOs, surprisingly enough, have much in common with apparitions. Both seem to vary widely in their degree of physical reality. Some UFOs don't show up on radar; others do. Some don't appear on film or video even when the camera operator is certain he got the image in frame. Some people are prone to sighting UFOs, and even know intuitively (or psychically) when the next sighting is due. Prior to the 1940s, UFOs were typically described not as saucers but as zeppelins or even airborne schooners, imagery consistent with the expectations and concepts of that era. All of this is more understandable if we see UFOs as intrusions from a different channel, which can be received by an altered state of consciousness, but which are so deeply strange that our normal mental categories can't accommodate them. To construct an intelligible personal reality that incorporates this anomalous input, we fall back on familiar images—zeppelins, schooners, saucers. What we're really observing may be something entirely different, something our minds just can't process.

Marian apparitions. Distinct from ordinary ghosts, Marian apparitions are sightings of the Virgin Mary. Some of these apparitions materialize at regular intervals and have been witnessed by large crowds. The vast majority of witnesses are devout Christians with a particular veneration for Mary. Quite possibly, an altered state of consciousness, prompted by intense religious feelings, allows people to perceive something outside their usual frame of reference; to make sense of it, they visualize the intrusive element in the familiar and comforting terms of their faith.

All this is interesting enough. But what would happen if consciousness were to find itself not merely tuning to a new channel, or to a confused overlap of channels ... but to the whole frequency range at once—the total, unobstructed spectrum of reality?

From this perspective, we might see a logic, a pattern, a wholeness, a meaning and significance to everything that had previously seemed random, accidental, and unimportant. This comprehensive overview, once glimpsed, could never be completely forgotten—but if we then returned to our normal brain-based mode of consciousness, with all its narrowness and limitations, we would be hard-pressed to prove our insights or even to put them into words.

Varying the analogy slightly, suppose that we were suddenly gifted with the ability to see beyond the edges of the visible light spectrum. A whole new world would open up for us, a world of infrared and ultraviolet wavelengths, of X-rays and microwaves, of radio waves and gamma rays. It would be the visual equivalent of Bucke's "cosmic consciousness."

And if we were then to return to using only our normal vision, could we adequately describe in words the colors and sights we'd seen? I don't see how. Our experience could not be translated into the terms familiar to other people, who are restricted to normal vision. Yet, in fact, normal vision perceives only a thin slice of the electromagnetic spectrum, and the other frequencies in the spectrum are no less real than the visible light frequencies.

We would, like St. Paul after being "caught up to the third heaven," despair that he "heard inexpressible things, things that no one is permitted to tell." How can mere human language convey, or mere human senses grasp, the ineffable?

Precisely this dilemma faced the hero of our next chapter—an extraordinary Victorian gentleman by the name of A. Square.

CHAPTER THREE: THE THIRD MODEL

A hierarchy of dimensions

OUR NEXT MODEL draws on Edwin Abbott's 1884 classic *Flatland: A Romance of Many Dimensions*. The Flatlanders are two-dimensional shapes who live on the surface of a sheet of paper. One day, our hero, Mr. A. Square, is lifted off the paper and into Spaceland, the realm of three dimensions. For the first time he experiences the dimension of height and is able to look down on Flatland from above.

What he sees would have been inconceivable to him when he was still in Flatland. For instance, he can now see inside a windowless Flatland house even if all the doors are closed. Why? Because Flatland houses have no roofs (there is no third dimension, hence no up or down). Mr. Square, hovering over the flat sheet of paper on which Flatland is drawn, can simply look down and see the interior of the house. It's very simple and obvious, but only if one has the perspective afforded by the third dimension.

When he returns to Flatland, A. Square excitedly tries to convey his revelation to others, but they regard him as crazy and try to lock him up. It doesn't work; having mastered the third dimension, he can escape from a locked room simply by elevating himself vertically and dropping down outside the room. (To the Flatlanders, he appears to dematerialize in one location and rematerialize in another.)

The book is a wonderful explanation of dimensions and geometry, as well as a sly satire on Victorian social mores.

The author insisted he never meant it as a metaphor for any spiritual or religious truth. Nevertheless, it can be used that way. Our existence in this cosmos can be compared to A. Square's life in Flatland, and our crossover after death can be compared to A. Square's abrupt elevation into the three-dimensional world of Spaceland. Just as he saw his old life from an entirely new perspective, so will we; just as his consciousness expanded to contain this new information, so will ours. And should we happen to be brought back to life after a near-death experience, we'll probably find it just as difficult as Mr. Square did to explain the truths we grasped—to package higher-dimensional realities in lower-dimensional concepts. We may also, like Mr. Square, find people doubting our message and even questioning our mental health.

In this model, multiple layers of reality exist simultaneously on different dimensional levels. What is hidden from the perspective of Flatland is visible to those with the perspective of Spaceland or loftier dimensions.

For the two-dimensional inhabitants of Flatland, the experience of physical shapes is limited to the perception of length and width. They can't imagine the third dimension of height, because they have no mental category for it. They would have to expand their consciousness in order to accommodate a 3-D experience of the world. As their "subjective" mental processing evolves, their experience of the "objective" world evolves with it.

In other words, the different planes of reality correspond to different levels of consciousness. The five-dimensional plane requires a higher level of consciousness than the four-dimensional plane. Environment and observer must evolve together. We could just as easily speak of higher-dimensional consciousness as we do of higher-dimensional reality. As with the frequency model, they are two sides of the same coin. Each higher level incorporates all the lower ones, with the highest level subsuming everything else.

To speak of going "higher" in terms of dimensions is also to speak of going "deeper" in terms of structure. Just as we use the terms *high* and *deep* interchangeably to refer to advanced thinking (a high-minded deep thinker, or elevated, profound thought), there is also no contradiction in saying that as we go higher, we go deeper. The highest level is also the deepest level, the ground of being.

Technically, our space-time reality consists of four dimensions—the three dimensions of space plus the dimension of time. But to maintain consistency with Abbott's book, in which time is not treated as a dimension, I'll refer to our cosmos—our experience of the world of appearances—as three-dimensional. The terminology doesn't matter, as long as we understand that higher-dimensional realms encompass the lower-dimensional ones.

Note that the two-dimensional world of Flatland is grounded in the three-dimensional world of Spaceland in the book. The ground of being, in other words, has more, not fewer, dimensions than the ordinary world.

How would four-dimensional realities be experienced in our three-dimensional world? If a pencil, a three-dimensional object, were to intrude into the purely two-dimensional world of Flatland, it would be perceived only as a slice. It might be a small dot (a slice of the graphite tip), or a somewhat larger circle (a slice of the wooden point), or a still larger circle (a slice of the shaft). Or, if the slice were made at an angle, then it might be an oval. If the pencil were sliced lengthwise down the middle, it would be a silhouette of the pencil. But no matter how it is sliced, the slice itself will always be two-dimensional, and someone unfamiliar with the three-dimensional world will be unable to visualize the complete three-dimensional pencil, much less imagine its origins or its purpose.

By the same token, we can't directly perceive or visualize a four-dimensional thing. In our three-dimensional world, it will come through as a slice, conforming itself to our conditions at our level of consciousness.

The basic point is that the ground of being is a four- (or five-, or more-) dimensional reality, while our ordinary experience is a three-dimensional reality. Attempts to apprehend intrusions of four-dimensional phenomena into our three-dimensional realm will inevitably distort the true nature of those phenomena. We can see only a slice of this higher dimension. In fact, *we ourselves*—as we currently exist in this incarnation—are only a slice of our true higher-dimensional selves. Where we make an error is in mistaking the slice for the whole.

The quantum realm is a higher-dimensional reality, which serves as the base of our reality. We perceive particles because the higher-dimensional photon or electron must express itself in lower-dimensional terms when perceived. When not perceived, it is a cloud of probabilities outside of space and time. Because higher-dimensional reality transcends space, entangled quantum entities can continue to affect each other across any distance of space. And because higher-dimensional reality transcends time, delayed-choice experiments will show effects that are seemingly retroactive.

When it comes to human experience, perhaps we can find an equivalent of A. Square's elevation to Spaceland in our nightly dreams—or some of them, anyway. I suspect that some dreams are higher-dimensional experiences altered and distorted into confused slices of lower-dimensional memory. The lower-dimensional memory may bear as little resemblance to the original higher-dimensional experience as a two-dimensional circle bears to a three-dimensional pencil.

Dreams are hardly the only such example. As we've seen, altered states of consciousness are associated with telepathy, apparitions, and experiences of cosmic consciousness like C.M.C.'s in Chapter One. In any of these cases, it could be argued that, like Mr. Square, we have temporarily shifted into a higher-dimensional consciousness that transcends our concepts of space, time, and reality. But the most obvious and dramatic alteration of consciousness occurs during the dying process. It's here, above all, that we would expect to observe a dimensional shift at work.

That's how NDE researcher Kenneth Ring sees it. In *Life at Death*, Ring argues that the entire near-death experience can be understood in terms of a fourth dimension. He writes,

> Most of us, most of the time, function in the three-dimensional world of ordinary sensory reality. According to the interpretation I am offering, this reality is grounded in a body-based consciousness. When

> one quits the body—either at death or voluntarily, as some individuals have learned to do—one's consciousness is then free to explore the fourth-dimensional world.

The bright light and higher intelligence often encountered in NDEs, in Ring's view, is our own higher self:

> The individual personality is but a split-off fragment of the total self with which it is reunited at the point of death. During ordinary life, the individual personality functions in a seemingly autonomous way, as though it were a separate entity. In fact, however, is invisibly tied to the larger self structure of which it is a part ...
>
> This higher self is so awesome, so overwhelming, so loving, and unconditionally accepting ... and so foreign to one's individualized consciousness that one perceives it as separate from oneself, as unmistakably other. It manifests itself as a brilliant golden light, but it is actually oneself, in a higher form, that one is seeing ...
>
> The higher self, furthermore, has total knowledge of the individual personality, both past and future. That is why, when it is experienced as a voice, it seems to be an "all-knowing" one (to use the phrase of one respondent). That is why it can initiate a life review and, in addition, provide a preview of an individual's life and events.

Ring points out that the classic NDE "is one in which the concepts of time and space have no meaning." To illustrate this point, he quotes Carl Jung's account of his own NDE: "I can describe the experience only as the ecstasy of a non-temporal state in which present, past and future are one. Everything that happens in time had been brought together into a concrete whole. Nothing was distributed over time, nothing could be measured by temporal concepts ... One is interwoven into an indescribable whole yet observes it with complete objectivity."

The "world of light" or Summerland described in rapturous terms by many NDErs is, for Ring, a higher-dimensional realm constructed out of the thoughts and images of individual minds—another "world of appearances," he says, but "at the same time, this world of appearances is fully 'real' (just as our physical world is real); it is just that reality is relative to one's state of consciousness."

All of this is perfectly consistent with not only the dimensional model, but also the frequency model and the virtual-reality model (the latter, as noted, has many similarities to the holographic model, which Ring also draws upon). Again, the purpose of these models is to provide ways of making sense of the evidence, not to develop a definitive and exclusive explanation.

The divide between our ordinary state of awareness and the awesome near omniscience of the higher self can seem like an unbridgeable gulf. But perhaps we can make more progress toward this higher-dimensional consciousness even in our ordinary lives.

In *Changes of Mind: A Holonomic Theory of the Evolution of Consciousness*, Jenny Wade charts the development of consciousness from birth to death (and even before birth and after death). The most advanced level of the broadly conventional mindset (surpassing Egocentric consciousness and Conformist consciousness) is the dual stage of Achievement/Affiliative consciousness. Achievement consciousness is the outlook of someone who defines himself in terms of his job, earnings, and accomplishments. Affiliative consciousness is the outlook of the person whose life has meaning primarily in terms of relations with other people.

Can we evolve beyond Achievement or Affiliative consciousness? Indeed we can. Wade considers higher levels of consciousness in ascending order. Here are abridged versions of her descriptions:

Authentic consciousness

Primary motivation: Personal growth for its own sake

Ultimate value: Fulfilling personal mission, even if not understood

Attitude toward life: Calm, insightful acceptance of existential problems and constant flux; assurance without certainty that life is inherently meaningful

Perception of death: No fear of death. Death is unknown adventure, even if it is nonexistence

Concept of other: Very little ego-based distortion. True empathy. Respect for personal agency, diversity, and autonomy of others. Relatively free of enculturation and conformity to social expectations. Impatient with people who impede subject's personal growth

Correct option: The one that works best and feels right at the moment; as circumstances change, a new solution

Transcendent consciousness

Primary motivation: Transcending the egoic self to grasp the Absolute

Ultimate value: Unity with the Ground of All Being

Attitude toward life: Reverence and appreciation for life as the manifestation of the Absolute. Attachment to life in its manifest forms must be overcome

Perception of death: Physical death is unimportant except as an opportunity for greater unity. Ego death is ardently pursued through persistent practice

Concept of other: Appreciated for their participation in the Ground of All Being regardless of outward form. Great compassion for and identification with all life forms

Correct option: One that will enhance unity with the Ground of All Being

Unity consciousness

Primary motivation: None—simply living in the Ground of All Being

Ultimate value: None

Attitude toward life: Non-attachment

Perception of death: There is no death except cessation of the body. Everything is immortal and constantly transmuting, therefore there is no attachment to life or death because each contains the other

Concept of other: There are no others in the Absolute sense. Recognition of the bounded selves that exist in the material plane as multiplicities of the One. Non-attached appreciation and compassion for, and identification with, others who are perfect as they are but are also suffering from attachment

Correct option: Only correct options exist

The few adepts who are able to achieve Unity consciousness may be remarkably close to union with the total self, without all the fuss and bother of actually dying.

Those who have died seem, in some cases, to take a continuing interest in this world, at least for a while. Like A. Square hovering over Flatland, they appear to be able to look down on us from the elevated vantage point of a higher dimension—to keep track of our activities, even anticipate our future. Events that remain hidden in the future to us may already be clear to an awareness that is elevated above the limitations of time as we understand it.

As a very rough analogy, imagine an observer high on a mountaintop. Below, an army is making its way through a narrow defile. Up ahead, unknown to the army, an enemy force has gathered in the foothills, concealed behind boulders. Simply by virtue of altitude, the observer can predict with a high degree of confidence that an ambush will shortly take place. A higher-dimensional consciousness, enjoying the ability to "look down" on our Flatland, might enjoy a similar advantage.

In his 1973 memoir *A Venture in Immortality*, David Kennedy documents a series of after-death communications from his wife that indicate not only his wife's awareness of his recent activities but also some knowledge of his immediate future. On one occasion, he was riding on a train with the medium Albert Best.

> Albert put down his book and in his excited typical stammer which I had come to recognize as the indication that he was getting something, he said, "Ann is just behind me, she asked me to tell you about the slipper". I said nothing and Albert paused for a few seconds as he often does while getting a message right. Then in more confident tone and slower and louder voice, "When your wife's personal effects were brought back from hospital were there blue slippers. No wait. There was only one blue slipper, the other was missing."
>
> He continued in his confident tone as he seemed to see things more clearly, "Your wife is giving this as evidence, you understand? In your wife's toilet bag she says there were three complete sets of dentures which came back from hospital. She is also saying, Teresa. The same toilet bag had a blue container of talcum powder and a triangular small bottle of toilet water." Albert continued, "Your wife was with you this morning when you took out a large silk handkerchief and used it to wrap something in. This

morning before you left the house ... she is singing a song which you should recognize. She is singing 'C'est si bon'. She is going now but says as she goes she knows about the Royal Stuart tartan."

Here indeed is concentrated evidence. Nothing vague but precise facts, one after another. First the blue slipper. This evidence was completely accurate. One blue slipper only came back in Ann's effects from hospital, the other was missing.

There were precisely three complete sets of dentures in Ann's toilet bag returned from hospital ... The name, Teresa, is Anna's mother's baptized Christian name. She has never used this name since she was married ... The blue container of talcum and triangular bottle of toilet water was [*sic*] in the bag as described.

[Earlier] that same morning, in my home alone, I took out the only silk handkerchief I possess, a large white silk handkerchief and used it to wrap the microphone of my pocket tape recorder to protect it when I placed it in my traveling case. Albert had never seen this handkerchief at any time. "C'est si bon" was one of Anne's favorite songs which she used to hum. Finally, a week earlier Ann's mother and sister had brought had bought a Royal Stuart tartan large traveling rug as a cover for the sofa.

In a first-time meeting with another medium, Mrs. Constable, Kennedy obtained more evidence.

She began, "You are working on a book just now but I feel that you have got stuck. Leave it aside for the moment and tonight just try to relax and scribble down any ideas that come to you, for half an hour or so." Suddenly she stopped, as though interrupted by someone whom she could hear, but who was not audible to me. "What's that you say? It's a lady speaking, she says, 'Tell him not tonight because he has to go out tonight'." I replied that I had an afternoon appointment but that I was free this evening and intended to be at home. "Oh no!" was the reply. "She says you are going to get a telephone call which will change your arrangements in the next few hours."

Mrs. Constable continued, "There is a lady here comes [sic]—the lady who spoke just now—a lovely lady—very beautiful—especially her hair. She says, 'Tell him it was my teeth.' She had trouble with her teeth. She is very quiet—shy. She does this to her mouth (here Mrs. Constable put her hand over her mouth) as though she used to hide her mouth or her teeth with her hand."

I must emphasize how completely accurate this description is of my wife. She had a shallow palate and gums. For years of her life, until she died, she was plagued by the problem of finding dentures which were comfortable and even wearable. All together she had four sets of dentures at the time of her death. We used to have a private joke between us. She would say to me, "If I ever come back to you after I die, I'll just put my hand over my mouth and

> say, 'Remember my teeth'." ...
>
> At 12 noon, a few minutes after I arrived home, I received a telephone call from the [people I had an afternoon appointment with]. The call was to ask me if I would mind coming out in the evening instead of the afternoon.

Can the deceased really see events in the future? A fascinating series of experiments carried out by Charles Drayton Thomas, whom we met in the Introduction in connection with young Bobbie Newlove, suggests they can. Working, as before, with British medium Gladys Osborne Leonard, Thomas was able to elicit specific information about words and phrases that would appear in particular locations in tomorrow's newspaper—even when, in many cases, the typesetters at the newspaper office had not yet composed the relevant page.

In a test on March 16, 1920, at 2:48 PM, Mrs. Leonard said, "At the beginning of column one there is a name usually associated with the very early part of the Bible. [The communicator's] reason for getting it is that you have noticed that name particularly within the last few days." Thomas observed that, "The first name in the column is Adams. I had certainly been thinking, during the previous day or two of a Mrs. Adams who was an old friend of my parents." Adam, of course, is the first human name given in the Bible.

Thomas, a clergyman, was accompanied to this sitting by another pastor, who came anonymously. Mrs. Leonard produced information specifically for him. "Near the top of column two, first page of tomorrow's *Times*, is the Christian name of the lady who comes with this gentleman." This was correct. "Four inches from the top of the column," wrote Thomas, "was the name Anne Maria." The pastor's deceased wife had been named Annie Maria.

Mrs. Leonard: "Close to it is this gentleman's Christian name. These are close together, and, possibly within half an inch."

Again, this was correct. "The Rev. Frederick" appeared in the specified location; Thomas's friend, a reverend, was named Frederic (without the *k*). More predictions, nearly all of them accurate, followed.

A dozen such tests were conducted. In each case, Thomas was careful to mail Mrs. Leonard's predictions to the offices of the Society for Psychical Research before the newspapers came out. The level of success far exceeded chance. As a control, Thomas would routinely check at least ten other newspaper editions to see if the same names and details appeared; he obtained very few hits.

Results like these suggest that the higher-dimensional realm really is beyond time, as we understand it. Intriguingly, that's what some people who've been there and returned actually tell us.

Dying to Be Me is Anita Moorjani's powerful account of her NDE and subsequent "miraculous" healing from cancer. Her rapid and medically inexplicable healing seems to be well documented, and the NDE itself has many classic features while also offering a certain novelty. In a passage about her NDE, she writes,

> I reached a point where I once again strongly

> sensed the comforting presence of my father surrounding me, almost as if he were embracing me.
>
> *Dad, it feels like I've come home! I'm so glad to be here. Life is so painful!* I told him.
>
> *But you're always home, darling,* he impressed upon me. *You always were, and you always will be. I want you to remember that.*

Later she notes, "Time was completely irrelevant. It wasn't even a factor to consider, as though it didn't exist." In a subsequent passage she expands on the idea of timelessness in connection with reincarnation:

> The concept of reincarnation in its conventional form of a progression of lifetimes, running sequentially one after the other, wasn't supported by my NDE. I realized that time doesn't move in a linear fashion unless we're using the filter of our physical bodies and minds. Once we are no longer limited by our earthly senses, every moment exists simultaneously. I've come to think that the concept of reincarnation is really just an interpretation, a way for our intellect to make sense of all existence happening at once ...
>
> All time and space exist right now, and we're simply moving through it.

The timeless quality of the higher-dimensional realm makes it somewhat easier to grasp the idea of the life review, frequently reported in both NDEs and mediumistic communications. One such message appears in Jane Sherwood's book *The Country Beyond: The Doctrine of Re-Birth.* What makes this message especially compelling is that Sherwood's book was originally published in 1944, three decades before Raymond Moody's *Life After Life,* at a time when the idea of a detailed and comprehensive life review (a term Moody coined) was seldom if ever encountered. The closest most people would get was the notion that their whole life flashes before their eyes when drowning, but this falls far short of an NDE life review, in which you experience firsthand the effects of your actions on other people and judge yourself for having acted morally or immorally.

With that in mind, take a look at this message from Sherwood's communicator:

> As one begins to use the astral body and it grows in strength, the scenes and events of the past life begin to come vividly back in terms of their *feeling* content and in a manner never experienced before ... The impressions of people, events and acts which now come crowding back are far more real and comprehensive than when they were actually experienced. The difference in this presentment of the past is that included in it now is the reaction of other people. I find this difficult to explain. Everything that happens to you affects others as well as yourself and every event therefore has as many aspects in *reality* as there are consciousnesses affected by it. Each of these others concerned in these events had their emotional life altered thereby even though you

> were quite unconscious of what was being brought about by your agency. Now, in this process of recollection, as an incident comes back to one's mind it brings with it the actual feelings, not of oneself alone but of the others who were affected by the event. All their feelings have now to be experienced in oneself as though they were one's own. This means that the effects of deeds on the lives of others must be experienced as intimately as though to do and to suffer the deed were one. Where sorrow and wrong have been inflicted, sorrow and wrong must be *felt*, not merely known to exist ... We have to face the reliving of our whole earth experience in this way. (emphases in original)

The transition to a higher-dimensional state ought to bring about changes in perception even while a person is still embodied—most obviously, in so-called deathbed visions, which have been investigated ever since Dr. William F. Barrett published a short book about them in 1926. The most evidential deathbed visions are those in which the patient shows awareness of the death of a loved one, while having no ordinary way of knowing about it. NDE researcher Bruce Greyson compiled many of these cases for a 2010 article. The cases extend well back in history. One of them, written up in 1882, reports that a dying woman

> suddenly showed joyful surprise and spoke of seeing three of her brothers who had long been dead. She then apparently recognized a fourth brother, who was believed by everyone present to be still living in

> India ... Sometime thereafter letters arrived announcing the death of the brother in India, which had occurred prior to his dying sister recognizing him. (Greyson, "Seeing Dead People ...")

In 1885, Eleanor Sidgwick, one of the leading lights of the Society for Psychical Research, reported an interesting case involving a singer identified only as Julia X, who had been briefly employed six or seven years previously by an affluent lady. Now the employer was dying. On her deathbed she was coolly discussing business matters, when

> she changed the subject and said, "Do you hear those voices singing?" No one else present heard them, and she concluded: "[The voices are] the angels welcoming me to Heaven; but it is strange, there is one voice amongst them I am sure I know, and cannot remember whose voice it is." Suddenly she stopped and, pointing up, added: "Why there she is in the corner of the room; it is Julia X." No one else present saw the vision, and the next day, February 13, 1874, the woman died. On February 14, Julia X's death was announced in the *Times*. Her father later reported that "on the day she died she began singing in the morning, and sang and sang until she died." (Ibid.)

In 1899, Alice Johnson described the case of the dying Mrs. Hicks, who

> looked earnestly at the door to the room and said to

> her nurse, husband, and daughters, "There is someone outside, let him in." Her daughter assured her there was no one there and opened the door wider. After a pause, Mrs. Hicks said: "Poor Eddie; oh, he is looking very ill; he has had a fall." Her family assured her that the last news they had heard from him [her son, who was thousands of miles away] was that he was quite well, but she continued from time to time to say, "Poor Eddie!" Some time after she died, her husband received a letter from Australia announcing their son's death. He had suddenly become feverish the day of his mother's vision and was found dead, having fallen from his horse at about the time of his mother's vision. (Ibid.)

Some NDEs include this same preternatural knowledge of a recent death. In a 1968 case, a hospitalized woman

> perceived herself leaving her body and viewing the hospital room and saw her distraught husband and the doctor shaking his head. She reported that she went to heaven and saw an angel and a familiar young man. She exclaimed: "Why, Tom, I didn't know you were up here," to which Tom responded that he had just arrived. The angel then told the woman that she would be returning to earth, and she found herself back in the hospital bed with the doctor looking over her. Later that night, her husband got a call informing him that their friend Tom had died in an auto accident. (Ibid.)

In their 1993 book *Final Gifts*, hospice nurses Maggie Callanan and Patricia Kelley report the case of an elderly Chinese lady, terminally ill with cancer, who

> had recurrent visions of her deceased husband calling her to join him. One day, much to her puzzlement, she saw her sister with her husband, and both were calling her to join them. She told the hospice nurse that her sister was still alive in China, and that she hadn't seen her for many years. When the hospice nurse later reported this conversation to the woman's daughter, the daughter stated that the patient's sister had in fact died two days earlier of the same kind of cancer, but that the family had decided not to tell the patient to avoid upsetting or frightening her.

A case reported in 1995 by a medical doctor, K.M. Dale, centered on a nine-year-old boy, Eddie Cuomo,

> whose fever finally broke after nearly 36 hours of anxious vigil on the part of his parents and hospital personnel. As soon as he opened his eyes, at 3:00 in the morning, Eddie urgently told his parents that he had been to heaven, where he saw his deceased Grandpa Cuomo, Auntie Rosa, and Uncle Lorenzo ... Then Eddie added that he also saw his 19-year-old sister Teresa, who told him he had to go back ... Later that morning, when Eddie's parents telephoned

> the college, they learned that Teresa had been killed in an automobile accident just after midnight, and that college officials had tried unsuccessfully to reach the Cuomos at their home to inform them of the tragic news. (Greyson, "Seeing Dead People ...")

If the transition from life to death can be understood in terms of shifting to a higher dimension, perhaps the transition from pre-birth to birth can be understood as shifting to a lower dimension, a process that may not take place all at once. Very young children, with their imaginary friends and spontaneous sense of play, may still be in touch with their higher-dimensional home. This may help explain why a surprising number of children spontaneously report a past life, often providing vivid details that can be verified by investigators. This field of study, inaugurated by Ian Stevenson more than fifty years ago, is continued today by many researchers around the world. To date, more than 2,500 cases have been documented.

Carol Bowman's book *Return from Heaven* deals with reincarnation within the same (sometimes extended) family. One such case involves a small boy named Sam, as recorded in journals kept by his mother, Jodie. "Sam's first word was cousins," Jodie remembers. "Sam was obsessed with his cousins since he was a baby." He was thrilled to visit his four older cousins, whose parents were Molly and David. A few years earlier, Molly lost twin babies late in her pregnancy. Jodie continues her account:

> As he got older, Sam began insisting that Molly's

> family was his real family ... [Once] Sam burst into the room mad, hands on hips, extremely excited, and asked, "Why isn't Kevin [David and Molly's oldest child] my big brother?" I tried to stay cool. I explained to him that Kevin was his cousin, not his brother; Peyton was his brother. But Sam would not accept this. "Why isn't Kevin my big brother? Why are you keeping me here?"...
>
> Then one evening a few weeks later, we were all winding down before bedtime and Sam asked ... "Do you remember when Peyton and I were in your tummy at the same time?"

Jodie explained that this was incorrect; Sam was born first, and Peyton was born two years later.

> Sam got a blank look on his face ... then he started laughing with relief and said, "Oh, now I remember. You're wrong, Mom! We were in Aunt Molly's tummy at the same time and we didn't get born! ... Why didn't we get born, Mom? Why didn't we get born?" Then, before I knew it, he took off after his little brother, screaming, "It's all your fault! I told you I wanted to get born really bad and you didn't want to! Tell me how you took me out of there! ... How did you do that?"... Peyton pulled the pacifier out of his mouth, and his little face got more angry than I have ever seen it. He yelled at his big brother, "I wanted Daddy!"
>
> Sam fired back, "I didn't want Daddy, I wanted Uncle David!"

When things calmed down, Sam decided to "figure this out" and

> started counting on his fingers. "First I was in Aunt Molly's tummy and I didn't get born. Then I tried to get back into Aunt Molly's tummy but Sophie [Molly's youngest daughter] was there in the way. So I tried to kick her out ... and that didn't work, Mom! Then I got in your tummy and then I got born ... I sure did work hard getting here, Mom!" [A few moments later Sam] asked me, "Does Peyton always have to follow me every time I'm born?"...
>
> Sam told his little brother what he had just remembered. Peyton started laughing. To my surprise he seemed to understand completely. I sat there thinking, "These two are talking about something that happened long before they were born [and] they're acting like it's normal." ...
>
> Recently we were making a homemade birthday card for Aunt Molly. I asked the kids what they wanted me to write on the card ... Peyton said, "Tell her I was her blue baby and now I'm Peyton and now I'm red."

The twins, who had tragically asphyxiated because of a problem with the umbilical cord, were literally "blue" babies. Later, Molly showed Sam a picture of herself while pregnant and asked if he knew who was in her tummy. Sam immediately answered, "Me and Peyton."

Like A. Square, those who've been given access to a higher-dimensional reality find it difficult or impossible to put what they know, or how they know it, into words. Most cannot do much better than this little boy who, as a nine-month-old baby boy, suffered cardiac arrest during an emergency surgical procedure and was without a pulse for forty minutes. Afterward he was in a coma for three months. Kenneth Ring reports:

> When he was five, he was having lunch one day with his father and spontaneously brought up the time "when he had died."
>
> As the mother observed before she related this event to us, neither parent had ever heard this story before. She went on to say, "He had never, ever, been told that he had died. He was never told the things that happened to him."
>
> In any case, as the mother recalled the conversation, it went like this:
>
> He sat down besides his dad, and he said, "Dad, do you know what?" And his dad said "What?" "You know I died." "Oh, you did?" And he said, "Yeah." His dad said, "Well, what happened?" And he said, "It was really, really dark, Daddy, and then it was really, really bright. And I ran and ran, and it didn't hurt anymore." And his dad said, "Where were you running, Mark?" And he said, "Oh, Daddy, I was running up there [pointing upward]" ... And he said he didn't hurt anymore, and a man talked to him.

> And his dad said, "What kind of words did he say?" And Mark said, "He didn't talk like this [pointing to his mouth], he talked like this [pointing to his head]." Because he couldn't tell you with his little vocabulary that it was through the mind. And he said, "I didn't want to come back, Daddy, but I had to." (Ring, *Lessons from the Light*)

As in the case of Dr. Wiltse in Chapter One, the little boy seemingly had no choice about coming back. Kenneth Ring, in his discussion of NDEs as higher-dimensional experiences, looks at this "decisional crisis" and suggests that a choice is being made, but at a higher level:

> If the higher self does indeed have total knowledge of the individual personality, both past and future, that knowledge must include the "programmed" time of death for the personality. Thus, when an individual is told that he is being "sent back" or that "his time has not yet come," this presumably reflects the "life program" of that person's life. (Ring, *Life at Death*)

In *Near Death in the ICU*, Dr. Laurin Bellg quotes an NDEr's explanation of the element of choice involved in being sent back to life:

> I even tried pleading with her to let me stay. I told her, "It's my life, I should get to choose. I should have a say-so." Then she told me, "It's not that you

> don't get to choose. Part of you, in fact, is choosing and participating in this decision. It would be easy for you to choose to stay here, but you understand on a level you can't quite comprehend just now that there is more from your family relationships you need to experience and learn. And more they need to learn from you. When choosing is not an act of escape but an act of completion, then you will stay."

This line of inquiry implies a continuum not only of realities but of personal selves. Each of us, it would appear, is one part of a larger whole, one band of a wider spectrum, one slice of a higher-dimensional totality ...

Or one facet of a diamond.

CHAPTER FOUR: THE FOURTH MODEL

A diamond of many facets

THERE WAS A time when, on a regular basis, I practiced guided meditations, in which I tried to achieve a mild trance state and then asked questions of a "spirit guide." I was aware of the possibility—even the probability—that any answers originated in my unconscious mind. But because I suspect that the boundary between the unconscious mind and the spiritual realm is quite tenuous, and because a certain tolerance for ambiguity is necessary in carrying out these highly subjective experiments, I wasn't overly troubled about it.

At one point, when I was ill with sinusitis and running a slight fever, I had an unusually vivid, emotionally powerful, and convincing meditative experience. As I lay on the couch, drifting between sleep and a half-awake state, having eaten little all day, I asked what my soul was like.

What came to me was an image of a diamond, brilliant and multifaceted. But this was no ordinary diamond. It was *alive*. The luminous facets were in constant motion, shifting their positions like pieces of a mosaic, creating intricate and harmonious patterns. There seemed to be nothing random about these patterns; rather, they appeared to involve the working-out of some larger scheme, much as notes of music work out the themes and melodies of a musical composition.

I was told that this diamond was my true soul and the individual facets were merely contributing elements. The real me, the eternal me, was the diamond as a whole, even though

I wasn't aware of it in everyday life.

Each of these living and moving facets represented a persona that my larger soul had adopted in some previous (or perhaps future) incarnation. The group of personae added up to my true soul in its purest and highest form, or what we can call the higher self or the oversoul. This oversoul is very much more than any one facet of the diamond; it consists of all the facets and the core of the diamond as well. Thus we are much greater, much more all-encompassing, than we think.

What was most strongly impressed on me was the sheer beauty of the soul. It seemed to me that this soul was the most beautiful and precious thing in the world. Of course, I'm not just talking about my own soul, but about any human soul. The sense I had—and this is where the emotional impact came in—was that if each of us could only grasp the magnificence and perfection of our own soul, we would have a whole new perspective on life, and negative things (such as the illness I was experiencing) would pale into insignificance.

I came away with a conviction that the soul—mine, yours, or anyone's—is an object of exquisite beauty, unfathomable complexity, and ultimate perfection. Even the flaws we perceive in ourselves are not really flaws, but elements necessary to a larger harmonious whole.

There are many wonderful things in our physical reality, including stars and galaxies, but the message I got was that each of us, inasmuch as we represent this diamond-like perfection of the soul, is far more wondrous and valuable than any physical object.

I'm not claiming that any of this information was new to

me. The specific image of the soul as a diamond is part of the material attributed to a communicator called Silver Birch, channeled by Maurice Barbanell:

> What I have said is that the human individuality is not always a single entity but a facet of a larger diamond. These facets incarnate into your world for experience that will enable them to return to the diamond and add to its lustre and radiance ... [The individuated spirit] is a facet of a larger diamond to which it adds its contribution. (Riva, *Light from Silver Birch*)

The same basic idea has been expressed in other writings, notably the Seth material channeled by Jane Roberts:

> The soul or entity is itself the most highly motivated, most highly energized, and most potent consciousness-unit known in any universe. It is energy concentrated to a degree quite unbelievable to you ...
>
> You are one manifestation of your own soul ...
>
> Many individuals imagine the soul to be an immortalized ego, forgetting that the ego as you know it is only a small portion of the self ...
>
> Your soul, therefore, possesses the wisdom, information, and knowledge that is part of the experience of all these other personalities; and you have within yourselves access to this information, but only if you realize the true nature of your reality. Let me emphasize again that these personalities exist

independently within and are a part of the soul, and each of them are [*sic*] free to create and develop.

There is however an inner communication, and the knowledge of one is available to any—not after physical death, but now in your present moment. Now the soul itself, as mentioned earlier, is not static. It grows and develops even through the experience of those personalities that compose it, and it is, to put it as simply as possible, more than the sum of its parts ...

Now in terms of psychology as you understand it, the soul could be considered as a prime identity that is in itself a gestalt of many other individual consciousnesses—an unlimited self that is yet able to express itself in many ways and forms and yet maintain its own identity, its own "I am-ness," even while it is aware that its I-am-ness may be part of another I-am-ness. (Roberts, *Seth Speaks*)

Channeled by Geraldine Cummins, F.W.H. Myers says:

What the Buddhists would call the karma I had brought with me from a previous life is, very frequently, not that of my life, but of the life of the soul [in my group] that preceded me by many years on earth and left for me a pattern which made my life. I, too, wove a pattern for another of my group during my earthly career. We are all of us distinct, though we are influenced by others of our community on the various planes of being ... I shall not live again on

> earth, but a new soul, one who will join our group, will shortly enter into the pattern or karma I have woven for him on earth ... Here, in the After-death, we become more and more aware of this group-soul as we make progress. (Cummins, *Road to Immortality*)

Given that I was aware of all this from my previous reading, it's entirely possible that the image of the diamond was purely a product of my subconscious mind. Nevertheless, I would resist this conclusion. I've had only a handful of other meditative experiences that shared this same powerfully emotional quality, which I've come to recognize as a sign of a particularly intense insight. As best I can describe it, it's the feeling that my whole body is tingling with a pleasurable electric current and is suffused with joy, coupled with a sense of peace and acceptance, the sense that everything is all right and there is nothing to worry about, complain about, or fear. My teenage experience of something akin to cosmic consciousness, described earlier, had something of this same quality.

In any event, whether or not the diamond idea is literally true, it can serve as a useful metaphor or model, one that helped me work out something that puzzled me for years: the startling divergence between two sets of afterlife reports.

One set—call it Set A—is obtained largely from NDEs and mediumship. These reports typically have little to say about reincarnation and suggest that the earthly persona continues with a relatively limited widening of perspective immediately after death. The reports constituting Set B, obtained through hypnotic regression and the channeling of advanced spirits, insist on reincarnation and regard the earthly persona as a temporary role that is almost immediately discarded.

Set A focuses on an earthlike environment of gardens, parks, homes, and even cities, inhabited by beings in human form—the consensus reality of Summerland, built up out of homely memories. Set B tells of an abstract environment of pure geometry in which souls see each other primarily as glowing lights, with different colors of the spectrum relating to different degrees of spiritual evolution.

This divergence of reports bothers Stafford Betty, author of *The Afterlife Unveiled*, which collects some of the more prominent accounts of an afterlife experience (and which I'll be relying on for many of the quotes that follow). Professor Betty writes:

> I wish I could report that there was unanimity on [reincarnation], but the facts don't permit it. This lack is the main reason I leave open the possibility, however slight, that this entire literature could be coming from the subconscious beliefs of mediums rather than from spirits.

Here are some typical descriptions of the afterlife in Set A reports. The first series of messages comes from Raymond Lodge, who died in World War I and whose father, the prominent physicist Oliver Lodge, obtained many evidential readings. One medium reports that Raymond

> lives in a house—a house built of bricks—and

> there are trees and flowers, and the ground is solid. And if you kneel down in the mud, apparently you get your clothes soiled ...
>
> He says, my body's very similar to the one I had before. I pinch myself sometimes to see if it's real, and it is, but it doesn't seem to hurt as much as when I pinched the flesh body. The internal organs don't seem constituted on the same lines as before. They can't be quite the same. But to all appearances, and outwardly, they are the same as before. I can move somewhat more freely, he says. (Lodge, *Raymond*)

Asked if Raymond has eyes and ears, the medium replies:

> Yes, yes, and eyelashes, and eyebrows, exactly the same, and a tongue and teeth. He has got a new tooth now in place of another one he had–one that wasn't quite right then. He has got it right, and a good tooth has come in place of the one that had gone. (Ibid.)

In a passage that excited much ridicule when the book came out in 1916, the medium conveys Raymond's claim that even cigars and whiskey are available in the afterlife:

> People here try to provide everything that is wanted. A chap came over the other day, would have a cigar ... It's not the same as on the earth plane, but they were able to manufacture what looked like a cigar ... Some want meat, and some strong drink;

> they call for whisky sodas. Don't think I'm stretching it, when I tell you that they can manufacture even that. (Ibid.)

As mentioned earlier, if the postmortem world is constructed out of memories, then memories of cigars and whiskey are no more far-fetched than memories of houses and gardens, or of eyelashes and teeth.

The nineteenth-century medium William Stainton Moses once went into a trance and was conducted on a tour of the spirit world. He later said:

> I seemed to stand on the margin of a lake, beyond which rose a chain of hills, verdant to their tops, and shrouded in a soft haze. The atmosphere was like that of Italy, translucent and soft. The water beside which I stood was unruffled, and the sky overhead was of cloudless blue ... [Accompanied by a spirit guide, I] came to a road which branched along the foot of the mountain. A little brook flowed by its side, and beyond was a lovely stretch of verdant meadow, not cut up into fields as with us, but undulating as far as the eye could reach. We approached a house, very like an Italian villa, situated in a nook, amidst a grove of trees like nothing I ever saw before; more like gigantic ferns of the most graceful and varied description. Before the door were plots of flowers of the most lovely hues and varieties. My guide motioned me to enter, and we passed into a large central hall, in the middle of which a fountain

> played among a bank of flowers and ferns. A delicious scent filled the air, and the sound of sweet music, soft and soothing, greeted the ear. (Betty, *Afterlife Unveiled*)

An Anglican monseigneur channeled by Anthony Borgia is even more insistent on the highly physical nature of Summerland:

> We have no roads as they are known on earth. We have broad, extensive thoroughfares in our cities and elsewhere, but they are not paved with a composite substance to give them hardness and durability for the passage of a constant stream of traffic. We have no traffic, and our roads are covered with the thickest and greenest grass, as soft to the feet as a bed of fresh moss. It is on these that we walk. The grass never grows beyond the condition of being well-trimmed, and yet it is living grass. It is always retained at the same serviceable level, perfect to walk upon and perfect in appearance ...
>
> As we approached the city, it was possible for us to gather some idea of its extensive proportions. It was, I hardly need to say, totally unlike anything I had yet seen. It consisted of a large number of stately buildings each of which was surrounded with magnificent gardens and trees, with here and there pools of glittering water, clear as crystal ... Here we find broad thoroughfares of emerald green lawns and perfect cultivation, radiating, like the spokes of a wheel,

> from a central building which, as we could see, was the hub of the whole city. There was a great shaft of pure light descending upon the dome of this building, and we felt instinctively ... that in this temple we could together send up our thanks to the Great Source of all. (Ibid.)

Despite the appearance of physicality, Summerland is ultimately a creation of the mind—or more precisely, a collaboration among the various minds of the spirits inhabiting it.

As we've seen, the discarnate F.W.H. Myers called Summerland the "Plane of Illusion" (or sometimes the "memory-world"). According to him, its inhabitants

> hunger for the dream which is home to them ... They enter into a dream that, in its main particulars, resembles the earth. But now this dream is memory and, for a time, they live within it. All those activities that made up their previous life are re-enacted, that is, if such is their will ... The soul, freed from the limitations of the flesh, has far greater mental powers, and can adapt the memory-world to his taste. He does so unconsciously, instinctively choosing the old pleasures, but closing the door to the old pains. He lives for a while in this beatific, infantile state. But, like the baby, he inhabits only a dream, and has no knowledge and hardly any perception of the greater life in which he is now planted ...
>
> He bears within him the capacity for recalling the whole of his earth life. Familiar surroundings are his

> desperate need. He does not want a jeweled city, or some monstrous version of infinity. He craves only for the homely landscape he used to know. He will not find it here in the concrete sense, but he will find, if he so desires, the illusion ... It undoubtedly presents a more attractive appearance than his little grey London world, but in essentials it is of the same familiar stuff from which his England is made ... Nearly every soul lives for a time in the state of illusion. (Cummins, *Road to Immortality*)

I'm not insisting that all of these channeled messages constitute valid communications. Some may be garbled, subconsciously embellished by the medium, or simply fraudulent. But they are typical of the Set A material. They offer a surprisingly concrete, even mundane vision of the next world. Higher mysteries are as yet unexplored. Illusion, not reality, is the rule. And a person's consciousness is not greatly changed. A prominent judge, having passed over, has this to say:

> This is not a place where everyone knows everything—far from it. Most souls are nearly as blind as they were in life ... I am sorry to say that the person who has a clear idea of the significance of life is about as rare here as on the earth ... A man does not suddenly become all-wise by changing the texture of his body. (Betty, *Afterlife Unveiled*)

William Stainton Moses agreed:

> As the soul lives in the earth-life, so does it go to spirit-life. Its tastes, its predilections, its habits, its antipathies, they are with it still. It is not changed save in the accident of being freed from the body. The soul that on earth has been low in taste and impure in habit does not change its nature by passing from the earth-sphere, any more than the soul that has been truthful, pure, and progressive becomes base and bad by death. (Ibid.)

In Set A reports, reincarnation is either unknown or doubtful. Even a supposedly advanced spirit, communicating through William Stainton Moses, seems unclear on this point:

> There are still mysteries, we are fain to confess, into which it is not well that man should penetrate. One of such mysteries is the ultimate development and destiny of spirits. Whether in the eternal councils of the Supreme it may be deemed well that a particular spirit should or should not be again incarnated in a material form is a question that none can answer, for none can know, not even the spirit's own guides. What is wise and well will be done ... There are other aspects of the question which, in the exercise of our discretion, we withhold; the time is not yet come for them. Spirits cannot be expected to know all abstruse mysteries, and those who profess to do so give the best proof of their falsity. (Ibid.)

Now compare all this to a typical "between-lives" regression, part of the Set B material. Here, a patient of Dr. Michael Newton is hypnotically regressed to the point where she had just finished her last earthly life and had yet to commence the current one:

> Dr. N: As you continue to float along, what is your next major impression as you pass the spiritual gateway?
>
> S[ubject]: Familiarity ... People ... friends ... are here, I think ...
>
> Dr. N: All right, keep moving along. What do you see next?
>
> S: Lights ... soft ... kind of cloudy -like ... They are growing ... blobs of energy ... and I know they are people! ... Now I'm seeing half-formed human shapes–from the waist up only. Their outlines are transparent, too ... I can see through them ... There is only a trace of a mouth ... The eyes are all around me now ... coming closer...
>
> Dr. N: Do these eyes have the appearance of human eyes with an iris and pupil?
>
> S: No ... different ... they are ... larger ... black orbs ... radiating light ... I'm starting to recognize them–they are sending images into my mind–thoughts about themselves and ... the shapes are changing ... into people!
>
> Dr. N: People with physical human features?
>
> S: Yes. Oh ... *look*! It's *him*! ... (begins to laugh and

cry at the same time) I think it's ... *yes*—it's Larry—he is in front of everybody else—he is the first one I really see ... *Larry, Larry*! ...

Dr. N: Can you see them all clearly?

S: No, the ones in back are ... hazy ... far off ... but, I have the sensation of their presence. Larry is in front ... coming up to me ... Larry!

Dr. N: Larry is the husband from your last life you told me about earlier?

S: (subject rushes on) Yes—we had such a wonderful life together—Gunther was so strong—everyone was against our marriage and his family—Jean deserted from the Navy to save me from the bad life I was living in Marseille—always wanting me ...

[Newton comments:] This subject is so excited her past lives are tumbling one on top of the other. Larry, Gunther, and Jean were all former husbands, but the same soulmate. I was glad we had a chance to review earlier who these people were in sessions before this interval of recall in the spirit world. Besides Larry, her recent American husband, Jean was a French sailor in the nineteenth century and Gunther was the son of German aristocrats living in the eighteenth century.

Dr. N: What are the two of you doing right now?

S: Embracing.

Dr. N: If a third party were to look at the two of you embracing at this moment, what would they see? ...

S: They would see ... two masses of bright light whirling around each other, I guess ... We are

> hugging ... expressing love ... connecting ... it makes us happy ... (subject tightly grips the recliner arms) Oh—they are all here—I only sensed them before. Now more are coming closer to me ... *Mother*! She is coming over to me ... I've missed her so much ... Oh, Mom ... (subject begins to cry again) ... Oh, please don't ask me any questions now—I want to enjoy this ...
>
> Dr. N: (I wait for a minute) Now, I know you are enjoying this meeting, but I need you to help me know what is going on.
>
> S: (in a faraway voice) We ... we are just holding each other ... it's so good to be with her again ...
>
> Dr. N: How do you manage to hold each other with no bodies?
>
> S: (with a sigh of exasperation at me) We envelop each other in light, of course ... Like being wrapped in a bright-light blanket of love. (Newton, *Journey of Souls*)

Set B's souls exist not as recognizable human beings but as blobs of color. No eyes or eyelashes here, only "black orbs .. radiating light." Nor is there any mention of gardens and houses in most of these reports. Quite the opposite. Here's another hypnotically regressed subject, this one treated by Dr. Joel L. Whitton, recalling an especially intense session:

> I've never felt so good. Unworldly ecstasy. Bright, bright light. I didn't have a body as on Earth. Instead, I had a shadow body, an astral body, and I wasn't walking on anything. There is no ground and

> no sky. No boundaries of any kind. Everything is open. There are other people there and when we want to communicate, we can do so without having to listen, without having to speak. (Whitton & Fisher, *Life Between Life)*

Consciousness is elevated far beyond human terms, almost to the point of omniscience. A different patient relates the dying process as recalled under hypnosis:

> My body expands and fills the entire room. Then I'm flooded with the most euphoric feelings I have ever known. These feelings are accompanied by total awareness and understanding of who I truly am, my reason for being, and my place in the universe. Everything makes sense; everything is perfectly just. It's wonderful to know that love is really in control. Coming back to normal consciousness, you have to leave behind that all-encompassing love, that knowledge, that reassurance ... I used to be frightened of dying. Now I have no fear of death whatsoever. (Ibid.)

Souls plan their next incarnation, with full knowledge of all their previous life experiences:

> My plan was that I would pick a tragic event which would cause me to change my entire soul complexion during my thirties. By focusing on this event, I would search with whatever means were at

> my disposal to find deeper meaning in my life. This is exactly what has happened. (Ibid.)

The hypnotized subjects of the therapists who've studied this "interlife" phase of existence agree that such planning is not done in solitude. The higher self works in cooperation with other oversouls, who constitute a soul group—a collective of literal soul mates who progress together, often showing up as personae in each other's lives. One patient told Dr. Whitton:

> I am being helped to work out the next life so that I could face whatever difficulties come my way. I don't want to take the responsibility because I feel that I don't have the strength. But I know we have to be given obstacles in order to overcome those obstacles—to become stronger, more aware, more evolved, more responsible.

As Whitton and co-author Joe Fisher observe:

> Planning for the next life is frequently undertaken in consultation with other souls with whom bonds have been established over many lifetimes ... Group reincarnation, in which the same set of souls evolves through constantly changing relationships in different lives, recurs frequently, according to Dr. Whitton's subjects. The "karmic script" often calls for renewed involvement with people who have figured, pleasantly or unpleasantly, in previous incarnations ...

> It would seem that the term "soul-mate" relates to an entity with whom one has purposefully reincarnated many times in the cause of mutual growth.

Another of Dr. Whitton's subjects said:

> There are people I didn't treat too well in my last life, and I have to go back to the Earth plane again and work off the debt. This time, if they hurt me in return, I'm going to forgive them because all I really want to do is go back home. This is home.

There is very little overlap between Set A and Set B. Occasionally you encounter a report with features of both, as in this passage from *Testimony of Light*, channeled by Helen Greaves:

> Whilst I was meditating in my golden garden, I found myself "transported" to ... a cluster of entities about a Teacher. Immediately I experienced a rise of consciousness, an upsurge of joy, a mingling of unity and harmony which coloured my whole being. I cannot explain this in any other terms, though I doubt whether they will have the same connotation for you. I knew this was right for me. I had come into my own. There was no definite acceptance, the entire operation was unobtrusive and simple, yet I had the conviction that all was well, that I was amidst my fellow-travelers on the Way.

Here we have expanded consciousness and a soul group, connected to a typical Summerland image of a "golden garden." But this is rare.

Given that the two sets of reports are so different, the easiest course of action would be to jettison one set in favor of the other. Set A has been much more extensively investigated and relies on multiple lines of inquiry (NDEs, OBEs, deathbed visions, mediumship). Set B depends on channeled material from purportedly high-level spirits, which is less evidential because it is not concerned with verifying the identity of the communicator, and on hypnotic regression, a field fraught with controversy because hypnotized patients can be influenced by the hypnotist and may confabulate. If I had to choose one over the other, I'd go with Set A. Still, I suspect there is some truth in each set ... but not the *whole* truth in either.

The discrepancy between them may arise because we can't help but think of the afterlife in our familiar terms of time and space. In contrast, our present model suggests that all the facets of the soul exist simultaneously, with the diamond as a whole corresponding to the totality of the self. In the diamond model, it's entirely possible for multiple versions of the afterlife to be true. It all depends on our focus—whether we identify with one facet or another, or with the diamond in its entirety.

Set A originates in the facets of the diamond corresponding to earthly experience and its aftermath, as do memories of past lives, which simply require shifting our focus to other facets.

Set B originates in an identification with the diamond as a whole, rather than any particular facet. The between-lives accounts reflect a higher level of consciousness, a more holistic consciousness, in which earlier incarnations are understood to be temporary personae. It's worth noting that hypnotherapists say only the very deepest stage of hypnosis can access these deeply buried memories.

In short, the being of pure light moving through an unearthly geometric environment is the higher self, while the recognizable human form moving through a garden paradise is the incarnate personality.

Let's carry this model a little further. Each facet of a diamond is a prism that refracts light. Now picture a diamond that glows from the inside, its light emerging through all facets. Since each facet acts as a prism, the light emanating from each will be different. If the core of the diamond is the center of our being, the light refracted through each prismatic facet is one particular individualized persona. It's all the same light coming from the same source, but bent and shaped in different ways.

All of this is going on at the same time, or more accurately, outside of time. Let's take another look at Anita Moorjani's comment, quoted earlier:

> The concept of reincarnation in its conventional form of a progression of lifetimes, running sequentially one after the other, wasn't supported by my NDE. I realized that time doesn't move in a linear fashion unless we're using the filter of our physical bodies and minds. Once we are no longer limited by our earthly senses, every moment exists simultaneously. I've come to think that the concept of reincar-

> nation is really just an interpretation, a way for our intellect to make sense of all existence happening at once. (Moorjani, *Dying to Be Me*)

While it may seem as though we are engaged in a long and tedious struggle to attain spiritual enlightenment, the diamond model, like Moorjani's insight, suggests *we have already attained it*—that, in fact, we never had to attain it, because it was part of us from the beginning. All levels of awareness are part of a single whole.

To make this clearer, consider the purely fictional case of a higher self and three of its incarnations—first as Redbeard, a Caribbean pirate in the 1800s; then as Jean-Pierre, a French Resistance fighter in World War II; and currently as Dave, an American physician who works for Doctors Without Borders.

As a young child, Dave remembers his previous life as Jean-Pierre. Young children are open to input from their higher self in a way that most adults aren't. Dave remembers Jean-Pierre's life, not because the Dave personality previously existed as the Jean-Pierre personality, but because both personalities stem from a common source, and the young Dave is in contact with that source.

It seems he is most likely to remember only the oversoul's most recent incarnation. He remembers Jean-Pierre, but not Redbeard. If each incarnation is a stepping stone to the next one along a path of continuous growth, it might be expected that the current personality would be most closely in touch with the last one. The Dave personality is, in certain respects, an outgrowth of the Jean-Pierre personality, which in turn is an outgrowth of the pirate Redbeard. In some cases, this outgrowth results in the carryover of specific personality traits; Redbeard and Jean-Pierre lived lives of action and danger, and Dave will do likewise when he ventures into war zones to heal the sick.

Children are most likely to remember a past life that ended abruptly, usually because of violence or the sudden onset of disease. Quite probably, a life interrupted represents a missed opportunity, which the new incarnation is intended to correct. Jean-Pierre, like many in the French Resistance, died young, before he could fully learn the lessons planned by his higher self; Dave represents a chance to complete this phase of the oversoul's education.

By age eight, Dave's past-life memories fade. As an adult, he has more limited contact with his higher self, connecting with it only in dreams and meditative states, when he receives intuitions and inspirations. This pattern holds true until he's injured in a combat area and undergoes a profound near-death experience, in which he finds himself, in his recognizable human body, meeting departed loved ones in a beautiful garden. The experience plays out this way because he is still identified with the Dave personality and not with his higher self.

At a certain point in his NDE, Dave encounters a being of light, which he first interprets as Jesus (a holdover from his religious upbringing) and then, more broadly, as God. Actually, the being of light is the higher self, the oversoul, which Dave misinterprets as an outside entity. He simply cannot imagine himself as part of this radiant superconsciousness, which is so far above his own limited awareness. But as the being of light draws nearer, he finds himself merging with it

—though only partially and temporarily. For Dave, this is an unforgettable experience. It feels as if he has merged with God, become one with everything, and attained infinite wisdom. In fact, however, he has merged—not with God—but with the totality of his own soul.

Sometime after his NDE, Dave goes to a hypnotist who puts him in a deep trance and regresses him to a point before his own birth. In that state he experiences a premortem existence before the Dave personality came into being. He is now identifying with the oversoul, the source of that personality. As a result, Dave's recollection of his between-lives existence differs from his NDE. In his NDE, he was still identifying with the Dave personality, so he experienced himself having Dave's body, meeting Dave's friends, and seeing religious imagery consistent with Dave's belief system. In his hypnotic regression, he is not identifying with the Dave personality but with his higher self, so he experiences himself without a human body and without Dave's personal characteristics. Instead he sees himself and his friends (who are other oversouls) as shapes of light in different colors, with a full recollection of their various incarnations, as well as a full memory of their between-lives schooling and associations.

When the hypnotist regresses Dave to an even earlier point, he remembers the lives of Jean-Pierre and Redbeard. But he reports those lives from a somewhat detached perspective, because he is still predominantly identifying with his higher self. He can look dispassionately on those lives and assess what he learned from them and what mistakes they made.

Continuing his spiritual exploration, Dave starts going to

mediums. He notices that a medium never says a given communicator is unavailable, having already reincarnated. If the diamond model is correct, we would expect all deceased personalities—such as Jean-Pierre and Redbeard—to remain in the spirit world; reincarnation involves the manifestation of a new personality extruded from the oversoul, not the recycling of a previous personality.

Through all this, Dave is learning that he is part of something larger than himself, which is in turn part of something still larger. His ego may resist this idea; it wants to be Mr. Big! His spiritual journey involves letting go of the ego by degrees and ascending to higher stages of consciousness.

Not coincidentally, by diminishing his attachment to the ego, Dave reduces his identification with the Dave personality and increases his identification with the oversoul, which he may experience, subjectively, as a witness who observes his thoughts and actions in the background—a "still small voice" that becomes apparent during those moments when he quiets his chattering mind.

Like Larry Darrell, the hero of W. Somerset Maugham's novel *The Razor's Edge*, Dave has embarked on a challenging journey. "It's a long, arduous road he's starting to travel," Maugham says, "but it may be that at the end of it he'll find what he's seeking." The author observes:

> The man I am writing about is not famous. It may be that he never will be. It may be that when his life at last comes to an end he will leave no more trace of his sojourn on earth than a stone thrown into a river leaves on the surface of the water. But it may be that

> the way of life that he has chosen for himself and the peculiar strength and sweetness of his character may have an ever-growing influence over his fellow men so that, long after his death perhaps, it may be realized that there lived in this age a very remarkable creature.

In a similar vein, Jenny Wade writes,

> Although many people who have attained enlightenment lead humble, sometimes cloistered or hermetic lives, the radiance, clarity, and love they emit —and their rarity in the general population—have caused them to be considered superhuman in the past. They are thought of as divine beings (e.g., Gautama, Jesus), saints (e.g., St. Francis, Kabir, Julian of Norwich), sages (e.g. Lao-Tzu, Al-Gahzzali, Judah Lowe, Meister Eckhart), and spiritual guides (e.g., Ramana Maharishi, Brother Lawrence, Patanjali). Esoteric traditions maintain that this condition—unitive consciousness with the Ground of All Being—is the potential and true state of all human beings ... : "Be ye therefore perfect, even as your Father which is in heaven is perfect" (The Gospel of Matthew 5:48). Rather than *super*human, it is *fully* human to possess clear insight, pure compassion, and, though they are not important, transcendent powers. (Wade, *Changes of Mind*)

The doctrine taught by these saints and sages is remarkably consistent in its broad outline. Aldous Huxley called it the "perennial philosophy." In his essay "The Minimum Working Hypothesis," Huxley reduced this universal creed to its barest essence:

> That there is a Godhead, Ground, Brahman, Clear Light of the Void, which is the unmanifested principle of all manifestations.
>
> That the Ground is at once transcendent and immanent.
>
> That it is possible for human beings to love, know and, from virtually, to become actually identical with the divine Ground.
>
> That to achieve this unitive knowledge of the Godhead is the final end and purpose of human existence.
>
> That there is a Law or Dharma which must be obeyed, a Tao or Way which must be followed, if men are to achieve their final end.
>
> That the more there is of self, the less there is of the Godhead; and that the Tao is therefore a way of humility and love, the Dharma a living Law of mortification and self-transcending awareness. (Isherwood, *Vedanta for the Western World*)

Summing up, Huxley writes:

> Atman, or the imminant eternal Self, is one with Brahman, the Absolute Principle of all existence, and the last end of every human being is to discover the

> fact for himself, to find out Who he really is. (Huxley, *Perennial Philosophy*)

Maugham's Larry Darrell tells us,

> "I wish I could make you see how much fuller the life I offer you is than anything you have a conception of. I wish I could make you see how exciting the life of the spirit is and how rich in experience. It's illimitable. It's such a happy life. There's only one thing like it, when you're up in a plane by yourself, high, high, and only infinity surrounds you. You're intoxicated by the boundless space."

Who knows how far Dave can travel? Or how far any of us can go? Perhaps all the way to Unity consciousness. In this state of mind, which is also a state of being, we may approach, as nearly as an incarnate human being can, the radiant splendor of the diamond.

EPILOGUE: THE I-THOUGHT

Breathing fire

WHETHER WE VIEW this life as an immersive first-person virtual-reality game, as one band in a spectrum of frequencies, as a sojourn in Flatland, or as a single facet of a diamond, and whether we view the afterlife as advancing to higher levels of game play, as tuning to a new signal, as rising into higher-dimensional space, or as accessing more of the diamond's radiant light, the bottom line is that our ordinary experience of reality is not the whole picture, but only a small portion of it.

In all four models, the space-time universe rendered by our subjective perception is the tip of the iceberg, with the other nine-tenths hidden from sight. Vast expanses of reality and vast realms of consciousness lie submerged beneath the surface, difficult for us to access.

Difficult, but not impossible, as mystics, shamans, mediums, and psychics have attested throughout history. In near-death experiences, or in a trance, or in a dream, or in a reverie, or when using mind-altering chemicals, we can sometimes make contact with these other planes of existence.

And even when we can't contact them directly, they may make themselves known to us by hints and whispers, the behind-the-scenes promptings of what F.W.H. Myers in *Human Personality* calls "the subliminal self." For Myers, the totality of our identity greatly exceeds the personal ego, and our subconscious (or superconscious) mind, far from being merely a storehouse of repressed feelings and buried memories, is the wisest and most creative part of us, constantly funneling creative solutions and moral guidance to our conscious minds, keeping us in touch with our higher self.

Just how does this all work? What is the relationship between our limited earthly consciousness and the higher consciousness of the oversoul? To get into this, we first need to think a little more about what consciousness is.

Consciousness implies both a subject and an object. The objects of consciousness include sensory input, mental imagery, logical reasoning processes, memories, imagination, feelings, and thoughts. Yes, even thoughts are objects, not subjects, of consciousness. What, then, is the subject? It is pure awareness—nothing more and nothing less.

Pure awareness is known in some traditions as the I-thought. In *The Advaita Worldview,* Anantanand Rambachan describes it this way:

> The I-thought is centered on an awareness that is permanently present, being timeless and self-revealing. Its content and nature are nothing but awareness, without which it has no existence or reality. When the I-thought, whose nature is limitless awareness ... is subject to ignorance, it identifies itself with the characteristics of the body, senses, and mind in notions such as, "I am short," "I am blind," or "I am unhappy." Liberation from ignorance occurs when the I-thought ... comes to understand its nature as limitless awareness ... A requisite of such knowledge is a calm and translucent mind in which

> the I-thought is able to understand itself as nonobjectifiable, illuminating awareness, distinguishable from the body, senses, and mind, relating to all of these as subject to object, and as identical with *brahman*, the non-dual ground of all reality ...
>
> All thoughts originate from and can be reduced or resolved back to the I-thought. The I-thought, on the other hand, can be traced back to its source in awareness, without which it ceases to be. Awareness, however, cannot be resolved or reduced to anything else. It simply is.

The I-thought is the universal awareness, the Mind of God, which branches out into countless individual minds. The light starts out pure and undifferentiated, but as it passes through a given prism, it takes on the qualities of the prism, alters its pattern, and becomes something unique. This unique light of consciousness as filtered through the prism is what we call the individual self.

Consciousness is an evolving dynamic process. Its objects are the matrix of information consisting of all the facts pertinent to us as an individual, all the events of our life, all of our physical traits, etc.—which collectively serve as the prism refracting the I-thought into a specific identity. What makes this bundle of data more than raw, lifeless facts—what "breathes fire into the equations," to again use Stephen Hawking's phrase—is the I-thought itself.

The individual self survives physical death because its basic constituents—consciousness and information—are nonphysical, rooted in the I-thought and its associated informational matrix. What we call our self, ego, or personality is only the I-thought entangled with a characteristic set of objects—distinctive memories, personal thoughts and feelings, recognizable habits of mind.

In the computational model, the I-thought is playing the game, and the informational matrix is the dataset rendered into an avatar (ego persona) and virtual environment (space-time cosmos).

In the frequency model, the I-thought adjusts its resonance to tune to a given band on the spectrum, and the informational matrix is the content of that frequency.

In the Flatland model, the I-thought perceives dimensional space, and the informational matrix is the particular dimensional level that is perceived.

In the diamond model, the I-thought emanates from the core of the diamond, and the informational matrix is the facet of the diamond through which pure awareness is refracted.

If these metaphors strike you as too cold or too abstract, try to imagine the emotional impact of breaking free of the particular matrix that defines your everyday persona and being reunited, even temporarily, with the pure, unobstructed totality of your highest self. Near-death experiencers enjoy a glimpse of this ultimate oneness when they briefly merge with the light.

In *Randi's Prize*, Robert McLuhan highlights these almost inexpressible feelings:

> Near-death experience researchers' studies are

> laced with copious quotations from individuals who are only too happy to describe something they may have kept locked up for years ... There's a palpable sense of awe in the firsthand accounts, of euphoria, exultation and mystery. Experiencers struggle to find superlatives to convey the colour, the beauty, the forms, the music—much of which, they insist, is ineffable, utterly beyond description ... People who relive the event in their imaginations choke up, grasping for words that will convey the enormity of it.
>
> Listen to these little excerpts, taken at random from extended quotes in Kenneth Ring's *Heading Towards Omega*:
>
> "If you took the one thousand best things that ever happened to you in your life and multiplied by a million, maybe you could get close to this feeling."
>
> "This wonderful, wonderful feeling of this light."
>
> "There was the warmest, most wonderful love. Love all around me ... I felt light-good-happy-joy-at-ease."
>
> "I can't begin to describe in human terms the feeling I had at what I saw. It was a giant infinite world of calm, and love, and energy and beauty."
>
> "As I absorbed the energy, I sensed what I can only describe as bliss. That is such a little word, but the feeling was dynamic, rolling, magnificent, expanding, ecstatic—*Bliss*." (emphasis in original)

Or consider this excerpt from an interview with Dr. Tony Cicoria, who nearly died when he was struck by lightning, and who came back from his NDE with a newfound ability to compose music, which he says is "downloaded" directly into his brain:

> When I was in the light, I no longer had any connection to previous reality, but yet my consciousness was absolutely racing, and I was absorbing all of the feelings that I was having of how wonderful this was and there isn't any negative thought, everything is positive thought and love and warmth and a great feeling. It was just incredible ... I realized, "This is the most wonderful thing that anyone could experience."

But even these accounts must fall far short of the truth. Any of us, taken up to "the third heaven" like St. Paul, would find ourselves tongue-tied upon our return, unable to express concepts beyond our language and perceptions. We might do no better than Nick Bottom in *A Midsummer Night's Dream*:

> I have had a most rare vision. I have had a dream —past the wit of man to say what dream it was ... The eye of man hath not heard, the ear of man hath not seen, man's hand is not able to taste, his tongue to conceive, nor his heart to report what my dream was. I will get Peter Quince to write a ballad of this dream. It shall be called "Bottom's Dream" because it hath no bottom.

And yet there's more.

The ego is merely one persona out of many, one avatar in the game, one channel on the spectrum, one level of a multidimensional reality, one refraction of the light of the I-thought through one particular prismatic facet of the diamond. All of the game's source code exists at once; all of the channels are broadcasting all the time; all levels of reality are equally real always; the diamond's inner light passes through all facets simultaneously. What, then, is reincarnation? Not a linear process of the soul moving from one body to another, but the simultaneous intersection of many different informational matrices with the same essential consciousness. The result is a collection of individual selves that are distinct yet related, separated in space and time, but eternally together as one.

Now here's the tricky part. The diamond, existing outside of our experience of the space-time cosmos, is not bound by temporal linearity. What it will do, it has already done, and what it will become, it already is. The journeys undertaken by its component ego personae have all been accomplished, and the integration of all those personae into an unbroken whole is already done.

But the journeys were and are necessary to inform the whole. And the journeys were and are bound by linear time.

In other words, we can look at the situation from two very different perspectives—the perspective of linear time and the perspective of existence outside of time. And each perspective is correct in its own terms.

From a Flatlander's perspective, we are engaged in a long ongoing journey, but viewed from a sufficient height, the journey is already over. From the game player's perspective, we are in the midst of just one game, but in the source code, all outcomes already have been calculated and played out. And yet the journey must be undertaken, the game must go on, because if it is never commenced, it can never be completed. But having been completed, its commencement is preordained. All facets of the diamond have always existed, and yet it is only our struggle that brings them into being.

We could not exist without them, and they could not exist without us.

Confusing? Consider a Möbius strip. You can make one out of a paper ribbon; just give the ribbon a single twist, then glue the ends together. Place a pencil on the paper, and you can trace a continuous line that travels over both sides of the ribbon and returns to its starting point. The twist makes "both sides" into "one side" and creates an endless loop—technically known as a "strange loop," for obvious reasons.

The strange loop shows up in such imagery as a snake swallowing itself or M.C. Escher's famous sketch *Drawing Hands*. The hands are drawing themselves; they could not exist unless they were drawn, and they could not be drawn unless they already existed to do the drawing. Which came first, the chicken or the egg? That's another strange loop.

In a strange loop, cause-and-effect form an endless bi-directional circle in which effect leads to cause and cause leads to effect. The end is implicit in the beginning; the beginning contains the end. All is one, and everything has already happened, and will happen, and is happening now. Like the time traveler who saves his ancestor's life and thus ensures that he will be born, the already perfected oversoul directs the journeys that make possible its own perfection.

And where are we, as individuals, in all this? It depends on whether we identify with the pencil laboriously tracing a line along the Möbius strip, or with the strange loop as a whole.

Even the oversoul is not the highest attainment of consciousness. As we have seen, it interacts with other oversouls, the members of its soul group, who work together, planning incarnations and arranging for their various ego personae to mingle in each other's earthly lives. Unlike Simon and Garfunkel, the oversoul does not sing, "I am a rock, I am an island ..." It is part of a tightly knit community of higher selves all striving for advancement and needing to advance together.

If each oversoul is a diamond, then a group of oversouls linked together is a diamond bracelet. Now picture an infinity of bracelets, strung from one to the next in an endless daisy chain that adds up to the full panoply of consciousness in all its manifestations and incarnations and evolutionary stages in all possible worlds. Such an inconceivable array would be the sum total of the universal Mind. It would be God.

We can say, then, that our higher self both is and is not God. And our present-day incarnate self both is and is not God. From a timeless perspective, in which everything has been accomplished, our incarnate self is part of our higher self, which in turn is part of our group soul, which in turn is part of God—and therefore our incarnate self partakes of God. But from a space-time perspective, our incarnate self is still busy informing and perfecting the oversoul; the game is not finished, the spectrum not fully explored, the higher dimensions untapped, the diamond's facets yet to be polished to a high shine.

Does this mean that ultimately, when we step entirely outside of linear time, we must lose our precious mundane self, our "I"? No. Nothing is ever lost. In the eternal Now, everything that ever was or ever will be always *is*. Does it mean that we surrender our memories of this life when we enter our next incarnation? No, because our multiple incarnations all play out at once; we are alive in the twenty-first century, and in ancient Rome, and in a lunar colony, and in the afterlife realm, all at the same time (because there is no time). Does it mean that our higher self is subjecting us to suffering that we would not have chosen? No, because the higher self is us; as the apotheosis of all our mundane selves, it can choose nothing that we haven't already chosen.

A man of eighty, looking back on his childhood, feels both a sense of continuity with the child he was and a sense of detachment from him; he both is that child, now and forever, and is not that child, whom he has long since left behind. He may feel sorry for some of the suffering the child went through, yet also glad about it, because it made him the man he is. The child would not have wanted to suffer, but the man knows better. And the child and the man are the same. (And yet different.)

But paradox by its nature is incomprehensible. Which gives us another paradox—we can understand only by the method of not understanding.

A dream that hath no bottom, indeed.

Ω

CHAPTER NOTES

Introduction

fell through an open grate on a Manhattan street: The facts of George Pellew's death are quoted from his obituary in the *Harvard Crimson*. James Munves (1997) argues that Pellew's death occurred under more sordid circumstances. He makes a good case that the location of Pellew's death was changed so he would not be linked to the real address, a cigar store that doubled as a gambling den. Interestingly, in one sitting Mrs. Piper produced the following by automatic writing: "other things I could not or would not have [my father] see, cigar checks ..." Munves explains, "'Cigar checks' were gambling chips, sold in the cigar stores that fronted for the upstairs gambling dens." Evidently Pellew was acknowledging that he did frequent gambling parlors while alive. Despite this, Munves is skeptical that Pellew was the communicator, arguing that Mrs. Piper read a sitter's thoughts.

To avoid any embarrassment to his family, Pellew's name was changed to George Pelham in transcripts and articles concerning the séances.

Pellew apparently made an appearance at a séance: To keep this book within manageable limits, I'm not dealing with the hypothesis of "super-psi," a.k.a. "super-ESP." Briefly, this hypothesis holds that mediums obtain their information by using ESP rather than communing with spirits. Proponents argue that the medium not only can read the mind of the sitter(s) quite fluently (even dredging up long-forgotten details), but can also read the minds of distant strangers, clairvoyantly see into safe deposit boxes, foresee future events, and so on. The medium's subconscious pieces together all this disparate information in real time, narratizes it, and assumes a convincing persona of the deceased to reel off the story. The super-psi hypothesis is hard to disprove, because it grants the medium almost unlimited powers.

Some writers object to the term *super-psi*, saying that "ordinary" psi is sufficient to explain mediumistic communications. (See Michael Suddoth, *A Philosophical Critique of Empirical Arguments for Postmortem Survival*, 2016.) I disagree. Psi or ESP, as measured in laboratory experiments, is flighty, erratic, and unpredictable—a "wild talent." The extended stream-of-consciousness monologues provided by the better mediums, such as Eileen Garrett and Leonora Piper—complete with gestures, mannerisms, characteristic jests and turns of phrase, and startlingly trenchant details—go far beyond anything seen in lab tests of psychics, as far as I know.

These arguments can get surprisingly technical and consume many pages. You'll find detailed presentations in the books by Stephen Braude, Chris Carter, and Alan Gauld listed in the Acknowledgments section under suggestions for further reading.

A DNA match was sufficient to convict Ruark: Details are disputed. According to Playfair and Keen, Jacqui Poole's DNA was found on a pullover that police retrieved from Ruark's trash. Other police officers say Ruark's DNA was retrieved from semen and skin found underneath the victim's fingernails. A BBC article reports that the conviction was obtained by DNA-testing semen left on an unspecified article of Poole's clothing found at the murder scene (not rescued from Ruark's dustbin). Since the BBC article states that Poole's body was found "semi-naked," I'm left wondering if the pullover perhaps belonged to her, and Ruark took it with him and disposed of it in his trash because it was stained with his semen. *If* this is true, the pullover was indeed the critical piece of evidence. It's frustrating that there can be disagreement over such a basic fact.

Chapter One

My summary of Eusapia Palladino's phenomena relies largely on Holms, *Facts of Psychic Science.*

Miss Z relocated to another city, and Tart let the experiments lapse: Although Tart did not replicate the study, he notes that another parapsychologist reported similar results, with a similarly frustrating conclusion:

"Stanley Krippner (1996) had a similar experience with a young man who reported occasional OBEs. He was tested for four nights in the laboratory with an art-print target in a box near the ceiling of the room. On the occasion when he reported having had an OBE, he gave a suggestively accurate description of the target, and had shown an unusual EEG pattern of slow waves (unlike Miss Z) about the time the reported OBE occurred. But then he went off to medical school before any further testing could be done." (Tart, *End of Materialism)*

---

the marginal status of shamans, medicine women, necromancers, and ghost hunters in most societies: Some people argue that this marginalization is a feature only of modern Western societies. But Hansen shows that shamans, etc., are marginalized in traditional societies, as well. There are taboos against occult practices such as spirit communications, unless conducted by the shaman, who lives apart from the community. The general attitude is that spirits are real but dangerous, and that it is safer to have nothing to do with them—not even to speak of them, except in euphemisms.
In other cultures, there may be a tradition of ancestor worship or other spiritualist customs, but these practices and beliefs are carefully compartmentalized, much like religious belief in the West.

People cite Brazil as a center of Spiritist activity, but statistically, only 2 percent of Brazil's population identify as Spiritists (about four million people, out of 210 million—although estimates vary). And this is probably the most openly spiritualist country in the world.

In general, it seems there is a pervasive undertow pulling human beings back to physical reality, regardless of their beliefs. Taboo, shunning, ridicule, compartmentalization, and amnesia all play a role.

---

descriptions of the Summerland: Good summaries of Summerland accounts are found in Betty, *Afterlife Unveiled.*

Quotes about salvia from various sources were originally compiled at michaelprescott.typepad.com/michael_prescotts_blog/2018/03/sally-forth.html .

---

like Melville's Ahab: In the full quote from Herman Melville's *Moby-Dick; or, The Whale* (1851), Ahab says, "All visible objects, man, are but as pasteboard masks. But in each event–in the living act, the undoubted deed–there, some unknown but still reasoning thing puts forth the mouldings of its features from behind the unreasoning mask. If man will strike, strike through the mask!"

---

the informational pathways are real at the computational level, but most of them are not actualized at the experiential level: In *The Hidden Domain*, Norman Friedman suggests that the quantum realm can be understood as consisting of complex equations–a mix of real numbers and imaginary numbers. Multiplying these equations by their cognates would give us real numbers only, or "physical reality." This process can be understood in terms of either mathematical calculations (multiplication) or wave interactions.

---

a world that is subjective but grounded in objective data: David Bohm's model of a holographic universe has much in common with this general approach. Roughly speaking, the informational field = Bohm's implicate order = Kant's noumenal realm, while the virtual-reality environment = Bohm's explicate order = Kant's phenomenal realm.

---

to be is to be perceived: *Esse est percipi* is the famous principle of philosophy George Berkeley.

"Those who are not shocked ...": Recalling a conversation be-

tween himself, Wolfgang Pauli, and Niels Bohr in June 1952, Heisenberg quotes Bohr as saying:

"Some time ago there was a meeting of philosophers, most of them positivists, here in Copenhagen, during which members of the Vienna Circle played a prominent part. I was asked to address them on the interpretation of quantum theory. After my lecture, no one raised any objections or asked any embarrassing questions, but I must say this very fact proved a terrible disappointment to me. For those who are not shocked when they first come across quantum theory cannot possibly have understood it. Probably I spoke so badly that no one knew what I was talking about." (Heisenberg, *Physics and Beyond*)

"condensed or frozen light": David Bohm's quote in context reads: "Mass is a phenomenon of connecting light rays which go back and forth, sort of freezing them into a pattern. So matter, as it were, is condensed or frozen light. Light is not merely electromagnetic waves but in a sense other kinds of waves that go at that speed. Therefore all matter is a condensation of light into patterns moving back and forth at average speeds which are less than the speed of light." (Nichol, *Essential David Bohm*)

Chapter Two

Without pressing the mechanical analogy too far: In telecommunications, the basic frequency of a channel is that of the carrier wave, while the informational content takes the form of an input signal imposed on the carrier wave. The input signal modifies (or "modulates") the carrier wave. The input signal is then extracted from the carrier wave by the receiver ("demodulation"). There are various ways of modulating the carrier wave, notably amplitude modulation (AM) and frequency modulation (FM).

Perhaps there is a way to incorporate modulation/demodulation into the frequency model we are exploring, but if so, I haven't thought of it. I suspect that any such attempt would press the analogy too far.

Anyway, for our purposes, the carrier wave can be forgotten; consciousness picks up the input signal alone. Ignoring the carrier wave isn't as arbitrary as it sounds; it's possible to transmit radio signals purely as input signals, without carrier waves. The practical problem is that an input signal is easier to receive when enveloped in a higher-frequency carrier signal.

Apparitions are much more commonly reported than we may realize: A Pew Research Center poll in 2009 found that 18% of Americans reported that they had "seen or been in the presence of a ghost."

---

in a medical journal: Dr. Wiltse published his case in the *St. Louis Medical and Surgical Journal* (November 1889) and in the *Mid-Continental Review* (February 1890). The case is also covered in the *Proceedings of the Society for Psychical Research*, (Vol. 8) p. 180.

---

only one of countless reports: For a comprehensive overview, see www.near-death.com/evidence.html .

Savants are people with neurological disabilities: This is true by definition. The majority of savants are on the autism spectrum, while a minority have suffered brain injury. According to William James's transmission model, the impaired brain, acting as a tuner-receiver, has trouble picking up the signal of our ordinary reality and seeks out a different signal. In terms of our own model, in which consciousness is the tuner-receiver, we might say that an impaired brain partially defeats the efforts of consciousness to tune to this frequency, with the result that consciousness, in effect, "wanders the dial" until it tunes in a clearer frequency.

———

the total, unobstructed spectrum of reality: The word word "unobstructed" reminds me of a classic work of channeled literature, *The Unobstructed Universe,* by Stuart Edward White (1940), which talks at length about frequencies of consciousness as the key to mediumship.

———

caught up to the third heaven: The quote from St. Paul reads: "I know a man in Christ who fourteen years ago was caught up to the third heaven. Whether it was in the body or out of the body I do not know—God knows. And I know that this man—whether in the body or apart from the body I do not know, but God knows—was caught up to paradise and heard inexpressible things, things that no one is permitted to tell." 2 Corinthians 2-4; New International Version

Chapter Three

The highest level is also the deepest level, the ground of

being: The fact that the Flatland model assumes that higher-dimensional realities are closer to the ground of being points to a difference with the model of a holographic universe. A hologram is a three-dimensional image projected out of a two-dimensional plate. In such a case, the ground of being has fewer dimensions than our observed reality.

Chapter Four

As uplifting as my meditative encounter with the diamond was, I can't say that its impact always stayed with me. As with my teenage epiphany, the memory has faded, as have the feelings the meditation evoked. For better or worse, our experience of the physical world is "fully immersive."

———

the carryover of specific personality traits: There can even be a carryover of *physical* traits closely corresponding to wounds or injuries sustained in the life of the previous personality. See Ian Stevenson, *Reincarnation and Biology: A Contribution to the Etiology of Birthmarks and Birth Defects* (1997).

Epilogue

struck by lightning, and who came back from his NDE with a newfound ability to compose music: Tony Cicoria is an example of "acquired savant syndrome," in which an injury to the nervous system results in previously unmanifested abilities.

———

technically known as a "strange loop": I was introduced to the concept of strange loops, also known as tangled hierarchies, in Amit Goswami's book *The Self-Aware Universe: How Consciousness Creates the Material World* (1995). However, Dr. Goswami employs the idea to somewhat different ends than I do here.

Paradox is the only way to understand it: Aldous Huxley writes in *The Perennial Philosophy*: "Whenever, for any reason, we wish to think of the world, not as it appears to common sense, but as a continuum, we find that our traditional syntax and vocabulary are quite inadequate. Mathematicians have therefore been compelled to invent radically new symbol-systems for this express purpose. But the divine Ground of all existence is not merely a continuum, it is also out of time, and different, not merely in degree, but in kind from the worlds to which traditional language and the languages of mathematics are adequate. Hence, in all expositions of the Perennial Philosophy, the frequency of paradox, a verbal extravagance, sometimes even of seeming blasphemy."

ACKNOWLEDGMENTS

I INVITE READERS to visit me at michaelprescott.net, where you'll find links to all my books, along with other neat stuff. I also invite you to drop by my blog at michaelprescott.typepad.com, where the topics covered in this book are regularly examined.

I've thought long and hard about how to acknowledge the many, many commenters on my blog who've helped me to examine and shape my ideas. I finally reached the conclusion that I would have to be unfair to most of them. It's just not possible to name them all, and any supposedly exhaustive list would inevitably leave people out. Instead, I decided to single out only a few longtime commenters whose ideas have been particularly influential with me, while apologizing for the omission of so many other valued names.

That said, special thanks go to Matthew Cromer, Eric Newhill, Matt Rouge, and the late Bruce Siegel. Bruce, by the way, was the author of an excellent study of precognitive dreams, *Dreaming The Future: How Our Dreams Prove Psychic Ability Is Real, And Why It Matters* (2017).

I also want to thank Michael Tymn and Robert McLuhan for their countless worthwhile posts on their own blogs. Many thanks also to Jon Beecher of White Crow Books for taking on this project and seeing it through. Finally, thanks to Diana Cox of novelproofreading.com for reviewing the manuscript and cleaning it up.

If you'd like to read further on the general topic of life after death, I recommend the titles listed in the Bibliography, as well as the following selections:

Overviews

STEPHEN E. BRAUDE, *Immortal Remains: The Evidence for Life After Death* (2003)

CHRIS CARTER, *Science and the Afterlife Experience: Evidence for the Immortality of Consciousness* (2012)

ROBERT CROOKALL, *Intimations of Immortality: "Seeing" that Led to "Believing"* (1965)

ARTHUR J. ELLISON, *Science and the Paranormal: Altered States of Reality* (2002)

ERVIN LASZLO & ANTHONY PEAKE, *The Immortal Mind: Science and the Continuity of Consciousness Beyond the Brain* (2014)

GREG TAYLOR, *Stop Worrying! There* Probably *Is an Afterlife* (2013)

Mediumship

ALAN GAULD, *Mediumship and Survival: A Century of Investigations* (1982)

BRIAN INGLIS, *Natural and Supernatural: A History of the Paranormal from Earliest Times to 1914* (1992)

MICHAEL TYMN, *The Articulate Dead: They Brought the Spirit World Alive* (2008)

——, *The Afterlife Revealed: What Happens After We Die* (2011)

Near-Death Experiences

CHRIS CARTER, *Science and the Near-Death Experience: How Consciousness Survives Death* (2010)

TITUS RIVAS, ANNY DIRVEN, & RUDOLF H. SMIT, *The Self Does Not Die: Verified Paranormal Phenomena from Near-Death Experiences* (2016)

MICHAEL B. SABOM, M.D., *Recollections of Death: A Medical Investigation* (1982)

Miscellaneous

D. SCOTT ROGO, *The Haunted Universe* (1977)

Skepticism

M. LAMAR KEENE, *The Psychic Mafia* (1976)

WILL STORR, *The Heretics: Adventures with the Enemies of Science* (2013)

The last two books take opposite approaches to skepticism. *The Psychic Mafia* is a famous tell-all book by a fraudulent medium who explains how he hoodwinked his credulous clients, while *The Heretics* includes a highly revealing interview with the most celebrated skeptic of modern times, James Randi.

BIBLIOGRAPHY

Books

LAURIN BELLG, *Near Death in the ICU: Stories from Patients Near Death and Why We Should Listen to Them* (2015)

STAFFORD BETTY, *The Afterlife Unveiled: What the Dead are Telling Us About Their World* (2011)

DEBORAH BLUM, *Ghost Hunters: William James and the Search for Scientific Proof of Life after Death* (2006)

CAROL BOWMAN, *Return from Heaven: Beloved Relatives Reincarnated Within Your Family* (2003)

RICHARD MAURICE BUCKE, *Cosmic Consciousness: A Study in the Evolution of the Human Mind* (1901)

MAGGIE CALLANAN & PATRICIA KELLEY, *Final Gifts: Understanding the Special Awareness, Needs, and Communication of the Dying* (2102)

MICHAEL CRICHTON, *Travels* (1988)

ROBERT CROOKALL, *More Astral Projections* (1964)

GERALDINE CUMMINS, *The Road to Immortality* (1932)

EVERARD FEILDING, *Sittings with Eusapia Palladino and Other Studies* (1963)

NORMAN FRIEDMAN, *The Hidden Domain: Home of the Quantum Wave Function, Nature's Creative Source* (1997)

JOHN G. FULLER, *The Airmen Who Would Not Die* (1979)

AMIT GOSWAMI, *The Self-Aware Universe: How Consciousness Creates the Material World* (1995)

HELEN GREAVES, *Testimony of Light* (1977)

MICHAEL GROSSO, EDWARD F. KELLY, EMILY WILLIAMS KELLY, ADAM CRABTREE, ALAN GAULD, *Irreducible Mind: Toward a Psychology for the 21st Century* (2006)

GEORGE P. HANSEN, *The Trickster and the Paranormal* (2001)

ERLENDUR HARALDSSON PHD & KARLIS OSIS PHD, *At the Hour of Death: A New Look at Evidence for Life After Death* (2012)

STEPHEN HAWKING, *A Brief History of Time* (1988)

WERNER HEISENBERG, *Physics and Beyond* (1971)

A. CAMPBELL HOLMS, *The Facts of Psychic Science* (1925)

ALDOUS HUXLEY, *The Perennial Philosophy* (1945)

CHRISTOPHER ISHERWOOD (ed.), *Vedanta for the Western World* (1985)

WILLIAM JAMES, *Human Immortality: Two Supposed Objections to the Doctrine* (1898)

DAVID KENNEDY, *A Venture in Immortality* (1973)

BRUCE H. LIPTON, PHD, *The Biology of Belief: Unleashing the Power of Consciousness, Matter and Miracles* (2008)

OLIVER LODGE, *Raymond or Life and Death* (1916)

W. SOMERSET MAUGHAM, *The Razor's Edge* (1944)

ROBERT MCLUHAN, *Randi's Prize: What Sceptics Say about the Paranormal, Why They Are Wrong and*

Why It Matters (2010)

RAYMOND MOODY, *Life After Life* (1975)

ANITA MOORJANI, *Dying to Be Me: My Journey from Cancer, to Near Death, to True Healing* (2012)

F.W.H. MYERS, *Human Personality and Its Survival of Bodily Death* (2001)

MICHAEL NEWTON, *Journey of Souls* (1994)

LEE NICHOL (ed.), *The Essential David Bohm* (2005)

DON PIPER, *90 Minutes in Heaven* (2014).

ANANTANAND RAMBACHAN, *The Advaita Worldview: God, World, and Humanity* (2012)

KENNETH RING, *Life at Death: A Scientific Investigation of the Near-Death Experience* (1980)

——, *Lessons from the Light: What We Can Learn from the Near-Death Experience* (1998)

PAM RIVA, *Light from Silver Birch* (2014)

JANE ROBERTS, *The Seth Material* (1970)

——, *Seth Speaks: The Eternal Validity of the Soul* (1972)

MICHAEL SABOM, *Light and Death: One Doctor's Fascinating Account of Near-Death Experiences* (1998)

JANE SHERWOOD, *The Country Beyond: The Doctrine of Re-Birth* (1969); reprint of 1944 edition includes material from *The Psychic Bridge* (1942)

CHARLES DRAYTON THOMAS, *Some New Evidence for Human Survival* (1922)

——, *An Amazing Experiment* (1936). Available at www.-

survivalafterdeath.info/library/thomas/amazing/contents.htm

Charles T. Tart, Ph.D., *The End of Materialism* (2009)

Darold A. Treffert, *Islands of Genius* (2011)

Rizwan Virk, *The Simulation Hypothesis: An MIT Computer Scientist Shows Why AI, Quantum Physics and Eastern Mystics All Agree We Are In a Video Game* (2019)

Jenny Wade, *Changes of Mind: A Holonomic Theory of the Evolution of Consciousness* (1996)

Joel L. Whitton, MD, PhD, & Joe Fisher, *Life Between Life* (1986)

Carl Wickland, MD, *Thirty Years Among the Dead* (1924)

Articles

Anon., "Obituary," *Harvard Crimson* (Feb. 23, 1892).,Available at www.thecrimson.com/article/1892/2/23/obituary-george-pellew-a-graduate-of/

Bruce Greyson, "Seeing Dead People Not Known to Have Died: 'Peak in Darien' Experiences,"*Anthropology and Humanism* (December 2010; Vol. 35, issue 2)

Richard Hodgson, "History of the G.P. Communications," *Proceedings of the Society for Psychical Research* (Vol. 8) pp. 295–335. Quoted in Myers, *Human Personality*

Chris Jones, "Roger Ebert's Wife, Chaz, on His Final Moments," *Esquire,* (December 2013). Available at www.esquire.com/entertainment/tv/news/a26606/

roger-ebert-final-moments/

JAMES MUNVES, "Mrs. Piper and 'George Pelham': A Centennial Reassessment," *Journal of the Society for Psychical Research* (Oct 1997, Vol 62, No 849)

GUY LYON PLAYFAIR & MONTAGUE KEEN, "A Possibly Unique Case of Psychic Detection," *Journal of the Society for Psychical Research* (Vol. 68, No. 874, January 2004) pp. 1–17

Online sources

ANON., "Beyond Death" (2019). Interview with Dr. Tony Cicoria. Available at superconsciousness.com/beyond-death/

TREVOR HAMILTON, "Gladys Osborne Leonard," *Psi Encyclopedia* (2018). Available at psi-encyclopedia.spr.ac.uk/articles/gladys-osborne-leonard

CLAUS LARSEN, "Birds of a feather: A 'special hit' does not hold water," *Skeptic Report* (no date). Available at www.skepticreport.com/birds-of-a-feather-a-special-hit-does-not-hold-water/

MR. PURRINGTON, "Carl Jung's Near-Death Experience," *Carl Jung Depth Psychology: Life, Work and Legacy of Carl Jung* (2020). Available at carljungdepthpsychologysite.blog/2020/02/03/carl-jungs-near-death-experience/

D. SCOTT ROGO, "Psychical Research and the Survival Controversy Part 3: Apparitions and the Case for Survival," excerpted from Rogo, *Life After Death: The Case for Survival of Bodily Death* (1986). Article available at www.survivalafterdeath.info/articles/rogo/apparitions.htm

MICHAEL ROHLF, "Immanuel Kant," *Stanford Encyclopedia of Philosophy* (2016) Section 3.1. Available at plato.stanford.edu/entries/kant/

BRIAN WHITWORTH, "The Physical World as a Virtual Reality" (2007). Available at arxiv.org/pdf/0801.0337.pdf

ABOUT THE AUTHOR

MICHAEL PRESCOTT has been writing suspense fiction for more than three decades. In his spare time, he maintains a blog dealing mostly with the paranormal and evidence for life after death. *The Far Horizon* is a result of his longtime fascination with this subject.

CPSIA information can be obtained
at www.ICGtesting.com
Printed in the USA
LVHW031350100221
678886LV00004BA/389

9 781786 771452